Applause and Accolades

Kathleen has developed unique ways to support aspiring authors to become real published authors. She has done it for me and for many of my clients too. I recommend her because what she offers really works. Find out for yourself in this thrilling book.

Raymond Aaron, Co-Author
Chicken Soup For The Parents Soul
-- New York Times Top 10 Bestseller

Chicken Soup For The Canadian Soul
-- Number One Bestselling Book in Canada
for ten weeks in a row after publication

I had no idea that I had actually already had the ideas and the outline for a book before I came to your workshop. The fact that you simply "turned on the light" in my head, made all the difference. Since then, the book is out, I have been asked to speak as an author at the Girls' school here and the book is on my co-author's Web site with international exposure. It would not have happened without that short afternoon I spent with you. Thank you.

Dr. Carolyn Anderson, Author
I'm So Mad I Could Throw Carrots at the Wall

Kathleen is a real asset in helping you build your book sales and business. She was instrumental in helping me brainstorm ideas for new titles, and making them happen quickly. Hire Kathleen today if you want to join the rank of self-published authors that live a life they love!

Troy White, Author
Million Dollar Multiples and *Entrepreneurial Spirits*

"YOU wrote a book?" is the question I get from everyone I know. *"YES! I wrote a book"* is the answer over and over again.

With Kathleen's book, guidance and intuitiveness, my journey began and in a very short time, I became an author. Everyone has a message and once you know what your message is, you will want to get it out there. With Kathleen's book, learning to write one yourself isn't a chore or a job, it's something that is totally yours to portray and share with everyone – it's actually a lot of fun and very easy. With this book, you are guided through the steps to ensure you don't miss anything. It's comprehensive, straightforward and very enlightening. It gives you so much confidence and a sense of power that you cannot resist the dream you have inside you to be an author – to be a successful author! Write your heart out!"

Live to Love

Debra A. Thomas, Author
FOR MEN'S EYES ONLY: The Ultimate Guide For The Romantically Challenged
www.hallofromance.com

I have just received my printed books! I have received so much support from Kathleen and the gang at Aurora Publishing! This is my first book and never thought I had a book in me... so, when I started writing it, with encourage-ment from my clients; I did not really believe I would actually publish it... then I met Kathleen and her team. I could not have done this, easily without them! And the quality of the work is impeccable! Thanks Kathleen and staff for all your ongoing support!

Rita Fipke, Author
Keep Your Sanity and Your Shirt

Kathleen Mailer is a mentor and coach. Her ability to understand and know a person's true gifts and being a mentor to help them attain their dreams is uncanny. Without Kathleen, I wouldn't have published my first book, "The Evolving Woman Series...Daily Reflections." I am now writing my second book.

Kimberley Langford, Author
The Evolving Woman Series...Daily Reflections.

Just the ONE idea alone you gave in that workshop has more than made me $1200 and I haven't even finished my writing my book. I have chosen to do this on my own but I can well see how a helping hand from you would make the process easier AND the prices you give are very reasonable. Just want to let you know that I appreciate the workshop.

Denise Gagne-Williamson

I was at your book writing workshop today and I just wanted to let you know that you really got my gears turning. To tell you the truth, I came into the workshop without any thoughts about writing my own book, but by the end, a light bulb turned on. I just wanted to share it with you and show you that you got through to me. I want to thank you again for giving me such an opportunity at this time in my life.

Shawn Grey, 18 years old

I never thought I could do it. Now I have 3 books and they just keep coming!

Madonna K. Girletz, Author
*Three Strikes And You're Out
The Making of an Independent Woman
The Dying Art of Teaching Your Horse To Do Tricks
30 Minute Home Spa*

I had been sitting on the thought of writing a book for 15 years and then took the "Kathleen Mailer's guide to writing" plunge! Her expertise and support was what I needed to actually start, write and later complete my first book. The thought to write more than one book never crossed my mind. But now that I have completed one, I have two others I will be starting.

Thank you Kathleen for your always positive support and insight.

Janet Holyk, Author
My Rose Coloured Glasses

Kathleen's words: "you have a moral obligation to get your message out to the world" slapped me good and hard. I realized she was right! The information in the workshop was so valuable and it led me to a life I have always dreamed of.

Monica Prochnaue, Author in Training

I used Kathleen's advice and I wrote my book in an afternoon!

Susan Blackwell, Author
101 Reasons to Be Optimistic for Life!

Sure to be a Number One Best Seller!

Networker News

How to Write & Publish Your Own Book

From Conception to Bookstore in 90 Days!

KATHLEEN D. MAILER

"Kathleen has developed unique ways to support aspiring authors to become real published authors. She has done it for me and for many of my clients too. I recommend her because what she offers really works. Find out for yourself in this thrilling book."

Raymond Aaron, Co-Author, *Chicken Soup For The Parent's Soul*, New York Times Top 10 Bestseller and *Chicken Soup For The Canadian Soul*, Number One Bestselling Book in Canada for ten weeks in a row after publication.

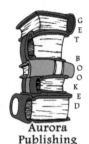

Aurora
Publishing

Soon to be Golden Gateway Publishing

A division of:
The Opulence Group of Companies Inc.
Calgary, Alberta, Canada
PH: 403-230-5946 ext 3
E-mail: opulence-academy@shaw.ca

How To Write & Publish Your OWN Book

Web site: www.kathleenmailer.com
Web site: www.howtowriteandpublish.com
Web site: www.yourchoicebooks.info

ACKNOWLEDGEMENTS

I would like to thank so many people on my team who helped me pull this together. All of you have made it possible to fill this book as full as I possibly could to help others and continue on my mission to make a difference in our world now, and for years to come.

Xenia, you did a great job editing this book. Your speed and dedication to get the job done is very dear to my heart. I thank you so much for everything you put into my projects - and make me look smart. ☺

Nik, you are amazing! Here you are making such a wonderful contribution and designing the layout and the book cover. I cannot possibly put into words how much your tireless drive has helped me, especially in the last few months. Having you on my team was, without a doubt, one of the best decisions I have made in a very long time. Your loyalty, friendship and kind understanding helped me have an even greater faith in humankind. Thank you for making me look good. ☺

Dan, you are not only my husband but you are my best friend, business partner and partner for life. Thank you for your encouragement when I didn't have courage. Thank you for your support when I didn't feel supported. Thank you for your willingness to learn new things, when I just couldn't do it all. Thank you for your commitment to us. Thank you for your belief in me. Thank you for being the father and head of the house to our loving family.

There really are not enough thank yous in the world to express the depth of my gratitude. For our readers' sakes I will leave it at this. Thank you for making me feel loved.

Dannielle and Sheya - Girls, thanks for supporting me and staying "out of my hair" when I needed to take time to write. You both are so amazing and I cannot wait for you to finish your books. Remember, you make a difference. The world is lucky to have you in it! Thank you for making me proud. ☺

And to you…. my dear reader……… YOU the Author…………

A Note To You - The Author

Congratulations! You have just changed your life!

There is nothing that compares to the excitement one experiences when you see your "baby" manifest into reality.

The things you will do and experience now will be much different than in the past! You have in front of you a whole new world, just walk through the open doorway to success. Who wouldn't walk through the doorway and walk on the path to abundance, fame, joy and financial freedom?

Unfortunately, I do know of some who wouldn't.

These are the people who have a hard time breaking free from their past experiences. People who bought the package and then LEAVE it sitting on the shelf beside all the other courses they bought in the past.

They get so caught up in everyday life they cannot look into the future long enough to hold their dream in front of them. If I describe you, it doesn't have to be so. Break free from these things that stop you from reaching your full potential. Call us and we will be happy to chat with you about it. Why?

BECAUSE YOU WERE MEANT TO BE ALL YOU CAN BE AND YOU CAN DO IT!

May your life be full of all the blessings you deserve. Respectfully,

Wishing you all of the best!

Kathleen

TABLE OF CONTENTS

SECTION ONE: GETTING STARTED!

Chapter One: 1
Oh Please, Why Should I Write a Book?

Chapter Two: 5
Setting Up This Business of Book Selling
 - Things to Consider When Setting Up Your Business
 - Merchant Credit Card Status

Chapter Three: 9
Creative Book Ideas, Tips and Thoughts So You Can Find
Out: How To Increase Your Business Bottom Line
 - How do I Pick a Title
 - What Should My Book Be About

★   ★   ★

SECTION TWO: THE WRITING BEGINS...

Chapter Four: 17
How to Crank Up the Creativity

Chapter Five: 19
52 Great Ideas & Topics for Writing Books and Articles

Chapter Six: 24
Book Writing Formula for Speed Writing

Chapter Seven: 27
How to Get Your Book Done in Record-Breaking Time

Chapter Eight: 28
Writing Your Back Cover Copy

SECTION THREE: THE PROCESS...

Chapter Nine: 31
13 Step Formula for Self-Publishing (An Easy Checklist Kit)

Chapter Ten: 32
ISBN Number

Chapter Eleven: 34
Cover Design

Chapter Twelve: 37
Book Size

Chapter Thirteen: 39
Pricing Your Book

Chapter Fourteen: 42
Manuscript

Chapter Fifteen: 42
How to Write a Children's Book

Chapter Sixteen: 46
Copyright

Chapter Seventeen: 47
How to Find the Perfect Editor

Chapter Eighteen: 49
A Word of Caution

SECTION FOUR: YOUR BOOK MARKETING PLAN OF ATTACK

Chapter Nineteen: 51
Who Will Invest In My Book?

Chapter Twenty: 53
How to Set Up, Create and Achieve a Mega Successful
Book Signing
 - Steps for a successful book signing

Chapter Twenty-One: 60
How to Get My Book Listed on Amazon.com

Chapter Twenty-Two: 61
How to Get My Book Listed in Chapters (CAN)

Chapter Twenty-Three: 62
How to Get My Book Listed in Barnes & Noble (USA)

Chapter Twenty-Four: 63
How to Get My Books Listed in Private Bookstores

Chapter Twenty-Five: 65
How to Set Up Consignment Agreements

Chapter Twenty-Six: 67
How to Sell My Initial 100-300 Books NOW

Chapter Twenty-Seven: 72
A Marketing Miracle, Making Money on Your Books BEFORE
You Have Them in Your Hands
 - 7 Steps You Can Take Right Now to Pre-Sell Your Book
   Effortlessly

Chapter Twenty-Eight: 74
Non-Traditional Markets to EXPLODE Sales

Chapter Twenty-Nine: 78
Attracting The Press
 - Press Kit
 - Sample Press Kit

★   ★   ★

JECTION FIVE: I AM OVERWHELMED; IJ THERE AN EAJIER WAY?

Chapter Thirty: 91
Let's Review
 - Self-Publishing Coaching Package

★   ★   ★

JECTION JIX: WHAT ARE JOME OTHER WAYJ OF JELLING MY WRITING?

Chapter Thirty-One: 97
How to Write Articles and Pitch Them to Magazines

Chapter Thirty-Two: 99
Become a Ghost Writer

Chapter Thirty-Three: 100
Become a Copy Writer

Chapter Thirty-Four: 101
Become a Columnist

Section Seven: BONUS: Million Dollar Directory At Your Fingertips

Chapter Thirty-Five: 103
Bookstores & Book Buyers Across Canada
- List of over 1500 bookstores and book buyers across Canada

Chapter Thirty-Six: 104
Libraries of the World
 - List of main libraries and their contact information for
   around the world

Chapter Thirty-Seven: 106
Book Fairs and Festivals to Sell Your Book
 - Book Fairs are a great place to sell your book or to get
   picked up by a big publisher.

Chapter Thirty-Eight: 109
Publishers
 - Comprehensive list of book publishers and their requirements should you decide to take your next print run to
   the publisher.

Chapter Thirty-Nine: 153
Magazines to Sell Your Work
 - Directory of magazines in a variety of different topics
   should you wish to sell your work in this way.

★　　★　　★

Section Eight: 32 Tips, Tricks and Techniques for Authors

Chapter Forty: 181

SECTION ONE:

GETTING STARTED!

CHAPTER ONE:

OH PLEASE, WHY SHOULD I WRITE A BOOK?

I meet so many highly intelligent, brilliant, dedicated and downright incredible people who haven't even begun to tap into the vast wealth of blessings that are waiting to be bestowed upon them.

There are entrepreneurs with a product/service that is second to none who are completely missing the income potential of thousands to hundreds of thousands of dollars in sales a year that they can easily incorporate into their business without a ton of effort.

There are coaches/public speakers I meet who are only doing "half" their job. They motivate their audience, then leave them high and dry - nothing to take home with them so that they can re-visit what they learned in that defining moment when this "angel" on stage switched on the light bulb in their mind.

There are struggling multi-level marketing directors/reps desperate to have a following. They believe in what they are doing, but haven't yet discovered the promised wealth. As a result of this fact, their credibility is on shaky ground. However, they must be doing something right! That "right" thing in their business needs to be released and taught. Let's face it, if you have 2 people who are in MLM rep/ directors' boots both vying for your attention - which one would you pick? Let's say they both have an equal amount of experience, they have equal "people" skills; however one of the two has written a book and as a result has been on TV and radio stations, and in newspapers. Who would you pick??

What about sales people? Realtors? Car sales people? Insurance industry agents? Again, this is a real no-brainer... Look at the facts! What puts you above the rest of your colleagues?

A Realtor could write a book called, *Cozy Up to the Fastest Sale in Town*... full of tips and ideas to help home-owners who are ready to put their house on the market sell their home quickly. Things like:

a) Clean up your closets
b) Bake cinnamon buns on the day of your open house
c) Turn on the lights
d) Place brighter/dimmer lights in the appropriate places, etc.

Professionals? Medical Doctors? Chiropractors? Massage Therapists? Lawyers? etc. Are you not responsible to educate your client in one way or another? Didn't you take some sort of sacred oath to do the BEST job you can? Teaching them, aiding them in their plight - write it down! Telling them details they need to know **in a book will not only help them, but will help you do your job more effectively**.

Who should write a book?
YOU SHOULD! (More about who should write in Chapter Three)

What is your excuse?

- **"I am too old!"** - Not true, I have several authors over the age of 65.

- **"I am too young!"** - Not true, children and young adults make some of the best-selling authors! I have had many come through the door and succeed.

- **"I can't write! I never received very good marks in high school English."** - So? You don't have to be a brainiac in English to write a great book.

- **"I have NO idea what I would write about!"** - That's the easy part!

- **"I never thought about being an author before."** - Now you can, and as a result, make all your dreams come true.

- **"I have a handicap."** - That shouldn't stop you from going for your dream! I have an author who is special needs. He has been on TV, on the radio and in papers. He personally raised funds for Fragile-X.

- **"What if I can't sell them?"** - There is a way to sell your books faster than saying "What book signing?"

- **"What if I can't get a book signing?"** - It is easy if you have a proven, step-by-step method. My authors have book-signings set up before they even have their printed books in their hands. It is as easy as that!

The truth is………
YOU CAN DO IT!

Who'd buy my book?
I think the better question to ask is, "Who wouldn't?" Hundreds to thousands of books can be sold before you even finish your book! It is true!

You can pre-sell them to clients, friends, family, associations, groups; at networking functions, tradeshows; as a back-end to any of your business dealings.

Excuses don't cut it!
Here's the REAL REASON why you don't/won't write a book!

**You don't know how to write and publish
your own book!**

There are mentors out there who would be happy to help you make it happen. Talk to other authors. Make your dreams come true NOW... don't wait!

You can start creating a brand new stream of income that will ease financial worries, bring you fame and create the life you have always wanted.

You will find your self-esteem will soar, your clients will look at you in a totally different light and your family members (as well as your friends) will be "wowed" by your success.

Chapter Two
Setting Up This Business of Book Selling

In my book, *Breaking Through Your Business Barriers!* I have a whole section dedicated to setting up your business. If you are brand new, you may want to pick up a copy of this book to help you with the process.

If you are not a newbie at business, then please just bear with me as I talk about a few quick details I feel are extremely important when starting a business venture.

Please remember this IS a business! The money you invest in this process is something you would like to recoup, I am sure. If this is the case, let me respectfully say this to you.

"ACT LIKE IT IS A BUSINESS!"

Quickly, here are a few details you will want to consider.

1. Decide on a publishing name. You will need this anyway, when you apply for your ISBN number (more about ISBN numbers later in the book).

2. Get your publishing company/trade name registered.

3. To be incorporated? Or NOT - That is usually the question I get. Please speak to your accountant or an authority on this subject to see what is best for you.

4. Have voice mail on your line! NOT AN ANSWERING MACHINE. Please, if you want booksellers and buyers to take you seriously, you have to seriously understand you need a professional image. A phone is your best friend and a very inexpensive employee.

5. Make sure your message is upbeat, personal and tells your callers that YOU are the person they want to have on their team. This can be as simple as smiling when you are recording your message. ALWAYS, ALWAYS, ALWAYS let your callers know the name of your book and where they can purchase it. Use it for advertising too! I can't tell you the number of people I have called who have a voicemail message that sounds like someone was standing in front of them drowning kittens. It is excrutiating getting through their voicemail. If you think that doesn't make someone run - THINK AGAIN. If you just can't get that energy up enough, ask someone else to do it for you. Also, one more item to mention. I can't tell you how many people comment on my voicemail about how they want to call me every day just to listen to my message. HMMM... Maybe there is something in this thing. Do you think?

6. Get an e-mail address. YES you must upgrade to the 21st Century! I know there are many authors who are not so computer literate. Many people argue with me that it just isn't something they need to do. I agree. You don't NEED to do anything. But if you want this to fly, you should have an e-mail address. Not only will you make many sales over e-mail but you will find the ease of getting your manuscript ready for your layout specialist and requesting things you particularly need much easier as well.

7. Have a dedicated FAX line so incoming orders can happen for you easily. There are many people, including myself, that will not take the time to phone and ask you to switch the FAX line on. Please don't short change yourself.

8. Another suggestion is to consider a Web site. There are places you could go to set up one that is author friendly. WARNING: not ALL Web designers are created equal. Please ask for referrals or find someone you trust. It does NOT have to be fancy! There are many one-page Web sites that rake in millions of dollars a year. You just have to make sure the person you hire is aware of this. It must have a way of paying online. This will make the cash flow into your business effortlessly.

Merchant Status - Taking Credit Card Orders

Here's why successful businesses accept credit cards:

- INCREASED SALES... Studies have shown that having a merchant account may increase sales by as much as 50% or more. Many direct marketing businesses produce 90% to 100% of their sales by credit card.
- LARGER CASH FLOW... When clients pay you with credit cards, you will receive your money faster than if you had to wait for them to send a cheque or money order.
- HIGHER PERCENTAGE OF IMPULSE BUYERS... With credit cards, buyers feel more freedom to make unplanned purchases.
- GIVES YOU A COMPETITIVE EDGE... Credit card users tend to seek out businesses that accept credit card payments over those that do not.
- ENHANCED CREDIBILITY... The ability to accept credit card payments gives you valuable credibility in the eyes of prospective and current clients.
- HIGHER PROFIT MARGINS... Credit card customers are typically less conscious of price differences than buyers who pay by cheque or cash.
- LARGER SALES... The average credit card user spends 2.5 times as much as cash buyers. YOU WIN!!

How do I go about getting set up?

1. PAYPAL: You can also use PayPal on a Web site. This is a convenient way of taking credit cards right away. Everything you need is just a "click" away. www.paypal.com

2. BANK: go to your bank and ask them if they will set up a Merchant account for you. This will take some time to complete. BUT, if you are processing many credit cards, it is a great way to go.

3. You can use a THIRD PARTY PROCESSOR to get your credit card status. Here is the information for the Merchant Processor we use. Let them know we sent you!

Bob Donegan, Senior Account Specialist
Bob@worldwidebilling.com
(800) 757-5453 EXT. 200
Int'l (509)-924-6730 Ext 200
(8:00 am -5:00 pm Pacific Standard Time)

- Accept all major credit and debit cards
- Process cards securely
- Highly competitive rates and transaction fees
- Back-end reporting, query and data tools
- Simple integration, with APIs for major platforms
- Technical support
- Capabilities to accept all major world currencies

We can process for U.S., Canadian, European and most International merchants. The approval time takes less than one week and, once approved, you will be set up the same day.

***Please note: This company is separate from Kathleen Mailer, The Opulence Group of Companies and any of its divisions. Please, as with any business decision, find out all your options and use your own discretion.

CHAPTER THREE
CREATIVE BOOK IDEAS, TIPS AND THOUGHTS
SO YOU CAN FIND OUT: HOW TO INCREASE YOUR BUSINESS BOTTOMLINE

Picture yourself standing in front of an audience in a large bookstore. The distinct aroma of crisp, fresh, new books wafts soothingly past your nose.

There is a tingle in the air and you can feel the excitement mount on behalf of the group who waits with anticipation for you to mesmerize and mystify them.

As you begin your talk, you notice the nods of the heads, smiles and tears forming as you connect with the whole room.

The standing ovation is short-lived only because they all rush to the till to buy their very own copy of your book!

Rushing, pushing and demanding an autograph of someone they admire and respect. They are thrilled at the fact they get to take a piece of a celebrity home with them.

- You swell with pride and purpose because you KNOW you made a difference here tonight.
- You KNOW you are on purpose.
- You KNOW, without a doubt, this is right for you.

As far as I am concerned, books are the number once choice a person has to share his/her message. Why?

- It is an easy, step-by-step approach that ANYONE can create.
- The process unfolds a huge dream in a relatively short period of time.
- The author experiences a sense of peace, satisfaction and pride.
- His/Her readers experience unparalleled serenity because they have the answer to their prayers.

In this chapter I will give you a special creative edge when you are contemplating what to write and what your title will be.

You will find a platform to have some ingenious thoughts manifest as how to actually write a quick book. AND, of course, I will lead you on a path to be inspired, inventive and resourceful.

Start Your Book Title With:

Use these title starters or come up with your own.

1. Discover the Secrets of...
2. How to...
3. 50 Ways
4. 101 Tips
5. A Step-by-Step Guide to...
6. 28 Steps to...
7. The Experts Guide to...
8. 30 Days to...
9. 90 Days to...
10. Brand New...
11. Cutting Edge

Other Title Words that Grip a Reader:

Be sure to have words in your title to reach out and grab your reader by the emotions. For example:

1. Survive
2. Outrageous
3. Tingle
4. Create
5. Fired!
6. Power
7. Failure
8. Success
9. Transform
10. Essential
11. Fool-Proof Method
12. Wisdom
13. Treachery
14. Sparkle
15. Reflections
16. Daily
17. Scandalous!
18. Vow
19. Privacy
20. Avoid

Book Ideas:

Keep your book simple. The above examples are great ways to create books fast. Check my Web site for some other ideas.

- "101 Tips" books are quick, inexpensive and simply an over glorified article you write. You can use them for FREEBIES. You can sell them, if you keep your price low enough. You can place them with another product/ service you currently have to add extra value.

- Inspirational books are always popular and in demand. You can create them as a "thought per day" book so your reader can plant a "good thought" seed in his/her head first thing in the morning or just before bed, that won't interfere with his/her jam-packed schedule. Use things like: a quote a day and follow it up with your thoughts and some questions to give your reader directions.

- An accumulation of theme articles. This is something many business owners don't realize they have at their fingertips. Books already written! FROM THEIR NEWSLETTERS! That's right. Just reconfigure it and VOILA... a book.

- Create new articles. If it is easier for you to write an article per day, in 30 Days you have written a book and it will be just what your readers want! Why? Because the biggest complaint the real world has out there is "I don't have time to read". With something like this, you take away their excuse and give them something they can work with.

- How-to books and manuals are the wave of the future. Everyone is trying to find the answers to solve a problem. If you send your how-to book out into the world, you are easily and creatively helping thousands.

- Children's books. Very popular way to reach a child's heart. They take the least amount of time and effort. Quick and effective to add back-end to anyone who is in any children's service.

- A Recipe or Cookbook

- Co-Author... gather interviews of people in your industry and make it into a book.

Who should write a book?
YOU SHOULD... look at some of the ideas below.
Where do you fit?

Multi-Level Marketing?
- Leader's guides
- How-to book
- Inspirational
- Meeting plans weekly - keep the speeches and turn them into a year long training book

Mechanics?
- How-to books, like "How to maintain your car so it lasts a lifetime".

Coaches, Trainers and Leaders... well this speaks for itself, doesn't it?
- What are you versed in?
- What subjects do you teach?
- How can this enhance what you are currently doing?
- Newsletters, Articles, Inspirational, etc.

Tupperware:
- How to: Save Money on Your Grocery Bill (benefits of proper food storage)
- Recipe book
- A Gourmet Kitchen How-to

Party-Lite Candles:
- How to Create a Stress Free Home Environment
- Decorate like a Pro How-To book

Mary-Kay:
- "Make Up for the Up Do Days, The Down Casual Days and the Around the Town Days"... (Ok... I just made it up... but there are a ton of How-To books you could write! Right??)

Teachers
- Children's books geared to your student's age group
- How-to books
- Manuals
- What about the reports, theses and creative writing projects you did in University?

Daycare workers
- Children's books
- A Parent's Guide...
- Sing-a-long books

Real Estate Sales
- How-to books
- Tip books on making a home show fabulous
- A recipe book... fit to sell your home!

Accountants:
- How to save money on your taxes
- Newsletter book of tips and ideas

Financial Services:
- How-to book
- Tip book on saving money - maybe even on your light bill, gas bills, etc. - and what to do with the difference

No matter WHAT your business is, you should add a book. Add a Little, Make A Lot.

Just before we move on, picture this...

You and your competition (I don't believe in competition but for the sake of argument let's pretend you have some):

- Both have exactly the same experiences in the industry.
- Both have been in it for exactly the same amount of time.
- Both businesses bring in exactly the same amount of money at this point.
- Both client lists have exactly the same number of clients...

Are you with me?

Now, you have written a book and next week you are on TV being interviewed by the morning breakfast show host. You have a great time for a few minutes and when you walk through the door into your office the phone is literally ringing off the wall! People who are your "perfect target market" are calling to ask you questions!

Whose business is going to grow? Yours? Or your competition's?

Who will get more referrals? You? Or your competition's?

Who will grow their business quickly? Increase their cash flow because they sold books BESIDES upgrading their readers to other products they have? YOU WILL!

Don't take this advice lightly. Isn't it time to make some changes in your life? You KNOW you are supposed to write a book - so just DO IT!

You now have several ideas. All you need to do now is create your book and get it ready to sell.

SECTION TWO:

THE WRITING BEGINS...

CHAPTER FOUR
HOW TO CRANK UP
THE CREATIVITY

If you have trouble getting into the "mood" to write, we often call it "writer's block".

The next chapter in this section will really delve into ideas to get over the hurdle.

Most of the time when writers can't get over this mountain, it is because they don't know how to explain things. If this happens to you, I have a few ideas to help you out.

1. Think this... "You know what? It is OK if I can't think of something." Give yourself permission to let it go. What happens to us when we want something SO BAD is that we end up hitting a wall of resistance. Just take a break. Perhaps you would like to go shopping. Window shopping is a nice lazy way to unjar the words.

2. Do something creative. Some people like to take pictures, play music, listen to soft CDs, dance, exercise. All will get the creative juices flowing.

3. Sometimes writing in your journal works like Liquid Drano to clear the drain. If you don't know what to write in your journal, start by writing down "starts" to a sentence and then filling in the blanks. Let me give you a few examples:
   a. I have writer's block because...
   b. I can't do this project because...
   c. I am afraid of this process because...
   d. I remember when... anything! This may be totally unrelated or seem to be, but you will be surprised ☺

4. Change locations. When I wrote the book *Leadership Wisdom From The Rock*, I went to Canmore, Alberta and rented a hotel in the mountains. I had writer's block and I used some of these tools. I went for a walk. It didn't help. BUT, when I opened my Bible it gave me some inspiration. It led me into what God wanted me to do. It helped me so much to bring things into perspective.

5. Meditation or Prayer opens up our channels to "see" clearly.

6. Visualize the book already done. See yourself on TV and doing interviews and picture yourself when you are doing that. Talk to a reader in your visualization and ask, "What is the most important message you received from this book?"

7. Cleaning up messes. Really and truly cleaning a mess creates a "void" in your cup of life. I talk about this in my program: Prosperity Matrix™ Series. When you are finished, think about what you do want, how you want your book to flow. It will help tremendously.

8. Maybe you do need a change. If you are writing a research book, change to writing some poetry or vice versa. This will help so much in the whole scope of things. It works the same way for me when I find myself engaged in heavy reading. I love to read and almost everything I read moves me through my life to a place of continual learning. Every once in awhile I need to stop and read what I call "fluff". A magazine or something like that gives me a chance to "breathe".

9. Write an article: Think about holidays, what can you write that will help you gather some tips for the holidays? Ask yourself, "What can I write about that will help others enjoy the holidays more?" How about "25 Stress-Free Tips for the Holidays"? For more information about this, see where we talk about writing for profit later in this book. Articles are fun and quick and exciting.

I hope this helps you crank up the creativity and crank up the fun in your life!

CHAPTER FIVE
52 GREAT IDEAS & TOPICS
FOR WRITING BOOKS AND ARTICLES

1. Compile 30 days of inspirational quotes and what they mean to you.

2. Write "101 Tips to Optimum Health".

3. Write a children's book.

4. Write an animal training book.

5. Write a "tricks and techniques" book.

6. Write a business book.

7. Don't forget to write a "series" of books.

8. Write a poetry book.

9. Compile a book of interviews with amazing people in your industry.

10. Write a book that announces new and innovative technology.

11. Write a book that announces quick money making ideas.

12. Write a book of financial tips.

13. Write a book of uses for vitamins and supplements.

14. Write "how-to" books.

15. Don't get ripped off! Write about how to find a trust-worthy _____ (mechanic, editor, manufacturer, multi-level marketing company, etc.)

16. Compile a book of short stories.

17. Write an inspirational story about yourself and how you made it to where you were going.

18. Write a murder mystery.

19. Write a romance novel.

20. Write a collection of short romantic stories.

21. Write a reference guide.

22. Write a "things to do" travel book for your city or area.

23. Create a magazine and then compile all the authors' articles into a book.

24. Create a book compiled from your newsletters or some-one else's newsletters (of course, with permission).

25. Write a parent's guide.

26. Write a children's guide to parents.

27. Write a book about tools of your trade, how to use them and where to get them.

28. Write a book on amazing facts.

29. Write a book based on historical events.

30. Write a biography of someone you admire.

31. Write a book containing instructions on card games.

32. Write a book that tells new parents how to prepare their children for school.

33. Write a book about the nitty gritty, down and dirty facts of _____ (you fill in the blank!)

34. Write a political book about all the parties and call it a Voter's Guide.

35. Compile a cookbook.

36. Compile a list book, example: List of all the business networking opportunities OR 50 home-based business ideas.

37. Write a homeowner's guide.

38. Write a how-to book on cleaning gutters.

39. Write a how-to book on landscaping.

40. Write a how-to book on babysitting basics.

41. Write a how-to book on certain types of legal advice (if you are not a lawyer - interview one or two!)

42. Write a how-to book on auto mechanics ... easy step-by-step maintenance. Again, if you are not an auto mechanic, interview one or two.

43. Interview Moms/Dads and ask them about the most heart-warming moments with their children. Have the book come out on Father's or Mother's Day.

44. Interview successful business people and ask them to give you the MOST IMPORTANT advice for new business owners.

45. Write a list of qualities you admire and explain why each is so important to life.

46. Write an advice book for new parents.

47. Write an advice book for new university students.

48. Write a daily JOKE book.

49. Write a list of humorous short stories.

50. Write a pet care book.

51. Interview teachers at your children's school and ask for solutions to common problems that children face at school.

52. Write a how-to book on art or craft projects.

Be creative! That is the most important thing. There are hundreds of things you are good at. You just need to find out who you are and then find others who are just like you. Share with them. Share with the world! YOU WILL MAKE THIS A BETTER PLACE.

I look forward to hearing some ideas from you.

WORKBOOK PAGE - YOUR IDEAS

_____

_____

_____

_____

_____

_____

WORKBOOK PAGE - YOUR IDEAS

_____

_____

_____

_____

_____

_____

_____

_____

_____

_____

_____

_____

_____

_____

_____

Chapter Six
Book Writing Formula for Speed Writing

This formula is an amazing formula for writing a book, developing a speech and creating articles. I think this is the most VALUABLE piece in this book.

You will be able to create an unlimited amount of product to sell if you use this formula. You can write books in 1-3 hours just like author, Susan Blackwell, Paul Larsen and many more.

The process is simple.

1. Get a pen and paper ready or sit down at your computer.

2. Think of a topic you wish to write about. Any topic in which you have expertise. A good rule of thumb is to think about your clients and what problems they are facing that you could solve.

3. Once you have that down, ask yourself, "If my client asked me for advice on this topic, what steps would I tell him/her to take?"

4. Write the introduction to your book. What you hope your readers will get out it. Talk about why you are writing this book then go on to the next step.

5. List the steps you would take. This becomes the chapter outline of your new book!

6. Once you have the outline of your book, fill each chapter by following this formula:
    a) State the step (chapter title)
    b) Explain what you mean by the step you were talking about
    c) Give an example of this explanation
    d) Give directions or ask specific questions to prompt a "response" from your reader.

7. Create a conclusion: This is where you will wrap up the steps and let your readers know what you want them to do now.

8. Follow our advice in the next section of this book to make the rest of the manuscript flow. That includes your acknowledgements, copyright page, etc.

Here is an example of what I mean you should do to make your chapters flow quickly. This topic is to help my professional speaking and coaching clients sell on stage.

I will answer the question: "Kathleen, how can I sell my book and products that we designed as back-end when I am speaking?"

The title of my book would be: "How to Sell Your Book or Products From Stage".

The introduction would delve into the topic of why you would do that.

The chapters of my book would look like this...
1. Understand Your Topic
2. Create a Keynote that highlights your product
3. Etc.

So when we do the chapter list it would look like this.

Chapter One: Understand Your Topic.
- I would then describe what I mean by this.
- I would give an example from my vast experience with hundreds of clients that explains this in great detail.
- Then I would give a direction by asking questions.

In what field are you an expert? It doesn't matter if you know someone who is even more experienced in the field or that there are a million other people doing the same thing. What counts right now is that you understand in what area you are an EXPERT. If you aren't an expert in a field, DON'T DO IT.

Make a list of the things you are qualified to teach. Get started on this list and continue to add to it. Ask your friends, neighbours, clients, colleagues what you are good at.

Keep your list close to you and then pick the one point you are passionate about! This will make you money. Passion equals cash flow.

Then I would go on to Chapter Two.

By the way, if you are interested in this new book, I couldn't wait to write it. I am doing that right now! Want a copy or more information? Go to my Web site at www.kathleenmailer.com and request a copy of this and other relevant information so you can sell from stage.

CHAPTER SEVEN
HOW TO GET YOUR BOOK DONE IN RECORD-BREAKING TIME

It is time now to focus. You see how easy it is to write the manuscript. It will be even easier to finish the project with the proper team of experts around you.

Here are some tips:

- Don't try and do EVERYTHING when it comes to your book. Book Cover Design, Layout, Manuscript Writing, Editing, etc. Pull together a team of experts.

- What if you do ONLY the part you are really good at? You can save yourself time and effort with the process. Trust me on this one. With my first book I tried to do every-thing in the beginning. I lost precious time and my job, compared to experts, was well, I guess I can't say this delicately - it really stunk! GET an EXPERT to help you.

- While you are writing your manuscript, your Cover Design Specialist can be creating your cover.

- Then, while your Editor is taking care of editing, you can be getting the ball rolling on printers and marketing for your book.

In a later chapter, I will give you a step-by-step guide to help you with the "flow" of your book publishing process.

Chapter Eight
Writing Your
Back Cover Copy

This is a very important part of your book. Next to the cover design itself, THIS sells books! The reader wants to know. What is in it for me? Why would I want to bother reading your book? What does this book have to do with my situation?

A great rule of thumb when writing a self-help book is to use the points you have made inside the book itself. If you followed the method we discussed for writing your manuscript, you gave the step-by-step process "to solve the problem" for your clients. List these steps on the back cover.

They will want your book because it has the steps listed AND it goes into detail on HOW to go about implementing it into their lives.

Also, in my book, *Breaking Through Your Business Barriers!*, I have discussed this in a little more length when I talk about making sure you aren't writing FEATURES when you should be writing the BENEFITS.

Features uncover wonderful aspects of your book. If it were a fridge, a feature would be: an ice dispenser.

Your clients might say, "that's nice" but they can also say, "so what?" to that statement. When you change a feature into a benefit you will want to ensure that you add a "so that you" into the sentence.

Let me give you an example:

"This beautiful fridge has an icemaker built right in (feature) so that you can enjoy an ice-cold glass of your favourite beverage on a hot summer day instantly." It is now a benefit.

If you make the back cover copy full of benefits, you will NOT be sorry. Think about this as you are writing your back cover copy.

Hire a copywriter if you need to. Remember your book is an investment. Treat it as such and it will be very good to you.

SECTION THREE:

THE

PROCESS...

Chapter Nine
13 Step Formula For Self-Publishing (An Easy Checklist Kit)

Here is an easy checklist for you to go through the step-by-step format of getting your book done.

1. Get your ISBN number, create a bar code for it and give it to your cover design specialist.
2. Come up with a subject and title.
3. Outline your book and start your manuscript.
4. Decide on cover design and get your cover design specialist on his or her way. Don't forget!
5. Decide on a book size, alert your cover design specialist.
6. Decide on the pricing of your book, alert your cover design specialist.
7. Write your manuscript.
8. Send your manuscript to the editor.
9. Source out your printers.
10. Finalize details on your cover design.
11. Ask for testimonials.
12. Set up book signings.
13. Create your marketing plan.

CHAPTER TEN
IJBN NUMBER

The International Standard Book Number is a 10-digit, soon to be thirteen-digit, number that identifies your book and e-books as legitimate published items.

What it does is identify one title or edition of a book from a certain publisher. It helps with the marketing aspects for libraries, schools, wholesale companies and other booksellers in their quest to match their market with your book.

This 10 or 13 digit number is a requirement of all bookstores. The letters ISBN precedes it and it is divided into four parts - each of different lengths separated by a hyphen. Basically it breaks down the country in which your book is published, publisher, then title identifier and finally what they call a "check digit".

Before your book is completed you can receive your ISBN number. When your ISBN number is presented on your book cover, it NEEDS to be in a special barcode. If you do not have a barcode for your book you can purchase the software or go to a barcode supplier. (Our authors go through us to get their barcode designed. For more information you can contact our office directly.)

Here is a sample of what the ISBN barcode looks like:

For USA: You can obtain your ISBN barcode at this website: http://www.isbn.org/standards/home/index.asp

For Canada: Go to the following website: http://www.collectionscanada.ca/isbndir/s11-202-e.html Fill out the order online.

Something to REMEMBER:

• Library of Canada needs two of each book.

• Within a week of your book being published you must send 2 copies of the book to the National Archives of Canada.

• The form can be found online at: http://www.collection-scanada.ca/6/25/index-e.html and then you will receive a receipt in the mail with a catalogue number.

CHAPTER ELEVEN
COVER DESIGN

This is a very important part of your book. First impressions are everything. We do judge a book by its cover.

Some basic tips to help you design your cover:

- Think of colour that stands out
- Not too busy, but not too plain either
- Front cover has the title, maybe one brief testimony, and the author's name
- Spine has the author's name, title of the book and publishing information
- Back cover should tell you what the book is about. (What is in it for your readers?)
- It should also have a testimony or two
- ISBN number
- Price of the book
- The reference section: e.g. leadership, business, spiritual, inspirational... where will the bookstore catalogue it?

Cover Template:

Refer to this template and be sure you have considered all the elements required for your cover.

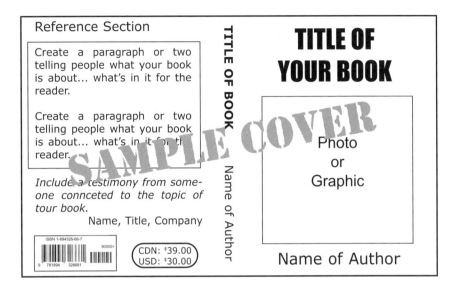

There is much to take into consideration when it comes to actually designing your cover. You need to consider the margin, the bleed of the pages, how big to make your spine, etc. The best one to talk to about these details is your printer, once again. He/she will help you with the measurements and tell you the specific program the cover needs to be in.

I have found it much easier to have someone else design the covers of my books. Over the years, I have become really great at "picturing" what it should look like and my graphic designer places it in our template that is already set up. She/he changes the colours, the font, the text, the graphics, but I don't have to worry about the details.

It can cost you from $500.00 - $1500.00 to get a cover designed for you. A good graphic designer is worth his or her weight in gold when you consider the frustration you may have trying to create the cover on your own.

I have met some fabulous masters in this industry who charge $4500-$24,000 US for this package. They are worth it when you remember your book is an investment.

Does it have to cost that much? If you don't know of anyone who has this expertise, please see section five for more help on this subject.

A good rule of thumb? If you are NOT a graphic designer and do not understand the basics of cover design, find someone else to do it. PLEASE. Also, I truly would like it if you remember, like all great art, it takes time to make your project beautiful. You really need to dedicate some time and effort in the creation of such an important part of your book.

Here are some thoughts and ideas that will help you and your designer create an amazing, powerful book cover:

1. What would you like to see on your cover? Is it a picture? Is it a cartoon?
2. What colour(s) would you like it to be?
3. Who will you get for a quick testimonial to put on the front cover?
4. What will the testimonial say?
5. What is the title of your book?
6. What goes on the spine?
7. Publisher/Title/Author's Name?
8. What testimonial(s) will you place on the back cover? And by whom?
9. Write a brief description for the back cover that will make your readers pick up the book and buy it!
10. What is your ISBN number?
11. Do you have the barcode design?
12. Under what category will your book be filed?
13. What is the price of your book (both US and CAN)?
14. Who is printing your books? Contact Name/Contact Information.

Chapter Twelve
Book Size

Your book can come in different sizes and shapes.

- The one size I found that fits very well is the standard book shape of **8.5" tall x 5.5" wide**. This works well because it is easier for printers to use as their template. As a result, the books are cheaper to manufacture.

- We also recommend our new mini book size: **6.5" tall x 5" wide.**

- Paperback novel size: **7" tall x 4" wide**.

- Children's book size: **7" tall x 9" wide**.

Other costs to think about when you are deciding on a book size:

a) Paperback is cheaper and perfect bound is better. A perfect bound is simply the same binding most books use. Coil bound is more expensive.

b) Colour versus black and white: while the cover is great to have in colour, it is very expensive to produce inside pages in colour as well. It is recommended you have a colour cover and inside pages in black and white. This will keep your printing costs down.

c) When you are perfect binding a book, page ranges can be effective from 32 pages all the way to 400 pages.

We use this size of book and these book guidelines to complete all our authors' works. We don't usually deviate unless the author wishes to pay much more for his/her copies of books.

Number of printed copies? Our suggestion is to go for a smaller print run. This is for many reasons but our prime reason is so you can get all the kinks out of your manuscript before you order 1000's of copies, then find out you hate your book!

Another reason for the smaller print run - it is much more cost effective and you don't have to lay out thousands and thousands of dollars, until you make some money with the books you already have.

You can use these books from the smaller print run to send out to publishers, media people and reviewers to help you increase pre-order sales.

The cost of this smaller print run? Depending upon the size of your book, number of pages (this price quote is for a book around 100 pages - this is NOT an exact quote - it is an approximate price range) and colour prints, the cost would be around $5.00 per copy on a 50 copies run PLUS setup fees. PLEASE CHECK WITH YOUR PRINTER FOR SPECIFIC QUOTES TO YOUR BOOK. This is just a "guestimate" to give you a place to start.

There is usually a one-time setup fee with your printer. Anytime you order more books after that, the cost will be only the printing costs.

Chapter Thirteen
Pricing of Your Book

Price goes on the back cover in USD as well as CAN dollars. A good rule of thumb, if this is your first book and the book is around 100 pages, is to charge: 100% mark up, at least.

What is the reason? Book buyers will charge you anywhere from 30-55%. This also gives you a measuring stick for those wholesale buyers that you will have.

It is up to you. Do your research. Remember what you have to say IS valuable. All the successful mentors in the industry say it doesn't matter if you are a little high on the bookselling price. It is better to be that, then undervalued. Just think about it. OK?

Chapter Fourteen
Manuscript

We will discover a few different things in this section of the book. We will talk about the different sections you can place in your book, what their purpose is and how you can arrange your book so you are not missing pieces.

We will also talk a little about your book layout and design. This is a very important piece so your reader can absorb your information effortlessly and easily.

What particular sections will go into my book?

This is personal choice but I will show you a list of the sections and what order they are usually in, in relation to your book.

1. **Testimonials:** Include many testimonials for your book. Sometimes these can take up to 2 pages of people telling your readers how great you or your book is and what they gained from it.

2. **Copyright and publisher page:** This has all the disclaimers in the book as well as your ISBN and copyright date.

3. **Dedication:** To whom would you like the book dedicated. This may be your parents, family or readers.

4. **Acknowledgements:** This page is to thank those you would like to acknowledge. This often includes those who helped make your dream come true.

5. **Foreword:** This page is a "large" testimonial. This could be written by someone of significance pertinent to the subject of your book,

6. **Preface:** Perhaps this may be looked upon as an introduction to prepare your reader for reading the book. Often this will have instructions for your reader - how you would like them to proceed. This is a great way to make a very long story short, to get them up to speed.

7. **Chapters of your book:** As many as you need...

8. **Conclusion/Summary:** If you require one.

9. **About the Author:** This covers a bit about you so the readers will be able to connect with you and also includes contact information. This helps them follow-up on your book and/or obtain more copies. Many people also put in another "ad" for their next book and/or other products and services they have to offer. This is why it is VERY IMPORTANT to give contact information.

If you would like a copy of our special report: How to Create A Book of Inspiration that will walk you through this step-by-step formula (like we have for a Children's book in the next Chapter), then go to our website at www.howtowriteand publish.com to claim your copy.

CHAPTER FIFTEEN
HOW TO WRITE A
CHILDREN'S BOOK

This concept is available in a Special Report. It comes complete with an example of a Children's Book in an eBook format. Please contact our office for more details or go to our website at www.howtowriteandpublish.com to order your copy today.

1. You can start by thinking of a story line suitable to the "age mix"
    • A general rule of thumb is ages as appropriate or grades. This depends upon your theme.
    • Don't forget that on your cover, usually on the back, you will want to mark down your "age" appropriation. This will help your readers identify with what they are looking for fast.

2. The writing of the manuscript is the EASY part. We will use an example for a story line for children ages 0-1 years old.

3. You will need to get your ISBN number for your cover design. Make sure it is in the proper barcode format.

4. The next thing you need to do is send your story to an editor. You may not think you need an editor but it doesn't hurt to have another pair of "eyes" look at your copy. It is very important that you help out your readers by making sure everything is spelled correctly and the text is understandable.

5. Before we talk about the illustrations part, you have to decide if you want your book in colour or in black and white. Colour is much more expensive to duplicate than black and white. You will need to talk to a printer about this and get a price quote you are happy with. Some books MUST be in colour, if that is your goal. Others can have sketches in black and white in order to create what you want to do.

6. Illustrations: There are many ideas for you to have your book illustrated. Here are a few:

   a) Take digital pictures; these can be produced in black and white with a colour one for your cover. This is what I would suggest for our small children's book we are going to create in this package. It is wonderful and fun to find the right pictures. This is also a great family venture for a summertime fun project.

   b) If you want sketches and need them to be in black and white, here is a wonderful idea that one of our authors sent to me. Go ahead and take digital pictures and pick up your FREE copy of this program. Look at this! This is from a digital picture!!!! Isn't that wonderful?? Go to Kodak Easy Share Software and search the site... excellent idea, eh?

   c) Find an illustrator. We have a few in our reference file who will help our authors create their packages. An illustrator can charge up to $1000 per picture.

> **TIP:** make sure you obtain the copyright for the ORIGINAL artwork. You should buy it completely outright so you can use the pictures in whatever way you wish. Of course, if you are an illustrator, then you can do the pictures yourself with less cost.

7. Contact the illustrator and send him or her your manuscript with a page breakdown in it. That is, where you do you want to pop in your pictures. Tell them exactly what picture you would like to place on the page. They should give you back a picture on letter size paper that can be scanned in and placed in your book. If your book is in black and white - then the pictures should be in black and white. Your cover should ALWAYS be in colour!

8. You will have to scan your pictures into the computer at a very high resolution. Your graphic designers, or layout specialists as we like to call them in our business, should be able to tell you exactly what you need. If they don't RUN... get someone who is highly qualified. You don't want to take extra time or effort when it comes to this process. You want it done right at the start.

9. Book Size: 7" x 9", usually saddle-stitched, unless it is over 32 pages, then it will be perfect bound. This is the general rule of thumb for paperback. If you have questions about special hard covers or you want to have it done in a unique format, it is best to go to your printers and ask for price quotes.

10. Once you have the pictures and manuscript back, send everything to your Cover Design Specialist and together you can create a masterpiece. Don't forget to give him/her your ISBN number!

TIPS:

• Think about a "series" with this process too. Can you create a series of books with the same character?

• Create a "growing up" phase of books. Start with 0-6 months and write a book for every stage of a child's life. Parents LOVE book series like this. They love collectibles for their child(ren).

- You can write a short story and turn it into a book.

- You can write about animals. Children can relate to bunnies and all sorts of animals.

Let me use our example below to show you the process as a "check list":

1. It is a picture book.
2. THEME: household objects. Apple, Chair, Clock, etc.
3. Book itself: small mini book, paperback, 32 pages in total.
4. Illustrations: done with my digital camera by myself.
5. One page will have the picture - the other page in big bold letters will have the "name" of the object.
6. Cover Design: happy baby on the front with her arms in the air with the words for the title: My Baby!
7. Back Cover Design: A house... with the word HOME similar to the inside of the book. It will have my publishing company, ISBN barcode, and price on the back of the book.
8. I have scanned in my pictures and sent it to my cover design and layout specialist who has put it into the proper format for the printers.
9. I have asked the printers for a price quote and have decided on how many copies I want to have in print.
10. I have checked with a mentor for the marketing portion and I am getting everything ready to go.
11. My book signing is now set.
12. My books are in and ready to sell.

Yes this process IS as easy as it sounds. Can you take the idea from above and do it yourself? OF COURSE YOU CAN. You can create anything you desire. Remember to use the steps we outlined and also to touch base with us should you need some help.

Chapter Sixteen
Copyright

This is a very important portion of your writing career. There are many things you need to think about, but this one is a top priority.

Copyright is a form of protection grounded in your country so no one can "duplicate" your material without penalty. Copyright covers both published and unpublished works.

It is also a form of intellectual property law and covers authorship for artwork, poetry, novels, movies, songs and so on.

1. You can protect your work without registration of copyright by simply placing the symbol ©, year, and your name on the material. Let me give you an example: ©2006 Kathleen D. Mailer
2. Then, mail a copy of your manuscript to yourself by registered mail.
3. Do NOT open the envelope.
4. Place the envelope in a safe place so if there is ever a reason, you can prove ownership rights.

Some people say you should register your copyright. This is up to you. Please go to the following informational website to help you learn more.

As any disclaimer, I must add that you talk to a lawyer and do a dedicated research of this subject in order to protect yourself fully.

USA: you can go to: http://www.copyright.gov
For Canadian copyright information go to:
www.bdc-canada.com

Chapter Seventeen
How to Find
the Perfect Editor

(Written by Melanie Morton - Editor Extraordinaire)

Your book is written, and it's ready to go - but is it really? You have checked, checked, and checked again for errors, but have you caught them all? Would somebody who had no clue what you were writing about be able to understand every one of your sentences? Hmm... maybe it is time to look into an editor...

What? You don't need an editor; you have spell check. Your husband/wife/friend... checked it over for you and it's fine? Let's look at some of the very compelling reasons to hire an editor.

1. It is a well-known fact that an author can only see some of his/her own errors. By hiring someone who is experienced in picking these errors out and correcting them, you are ensuring a higher quality product, thereby enhancing your own reputation... which could easily translate into increased sales!

2. Let's face it; we all know how poor the spelling and grammar checkers are at improving writing. They frequently suggest incorrect changes, and rarely catch such errors as missed words. They constantly mark correct English as bad grammar. No software can take the place of an experienced eye.

3. Editors will make your message clear, so that anyone should be able to understand the point you are making. They watch for spelling and grammatical errors; make suggestions for organization; and watch for other poor writing techniques, such as writing in more than one voice.

So, now you agree that you need an editor, how do you go about finding the right one for your manuscript? Here are some questions to ask that will aid you in making your decision.

1. Do you have testimonials?
2. What are my payment options?
3. What are your rates?
4. I have special projects (workshops, workbooks, marketing pieces, a website...) that will all need editing. If I hire you to do my book(s) AND my special ongoing projects, will you give me a volume discount?
5. How long have you been editing?
6. How many manuscripts have you edited?
7. How many hours will it take you to edit my book? Once I have sent it to you to edit, how long will it be before you have it completed and back to me?
8. Do you give estimates? If you take longer than expected, will I have to pay more?

Once you have asked all your questions, it is time to make your decision. The last piece of advice I have to give you is to use your intuition. If the match does not feel right, keep looking. You will want to have a feeling of trust, whether that comes from a personal referral, testimonial, or your gut instinct. YOU need to be confident in your choice.

Chapter Eighteen
A Word of Caution

Like everything else, you have to do your due diligence when you are finding a team to work with. Every person is in business for himself or herself and it is a good idea to keep the cost, quality and time frame in the forefront of your mind.

Research and "feel" really good about those you with whom you work. If they turn out to be as magnificent as I have for a team, then keep them. You will want to have a secure and solid base of people who surround you as you go through this process.

If they don't believe in you or make promises they cannot fill, then make sure you release the project and find some-one else.

Be reasonable and understand that things to do take time to make perfect. However, being reasonable with a timeline and having them "put you off" is a whole other ball game.

This is YOUR project and you want it done right or you won't be able to sell your books.

Your book is your investment, as I have mentioned before, make it turn out to be the best investment ever!

SECTION FOUR:

YOUR BOOK MARKETING PLAN OF ATTACK!

Chapter Nineteen
Who will Invest
In My Book?

This is one of the biggest myths I dispel every day in my career. Who will buy my book? Do you know how many books there are out there like this? Why on earth would someone want something like my story when there are more qualified people out there doing better things?

And the buzzer says,
"NEIIIIIIIIIIIIIIGGGGGGGGGGGGGGGGGGGGGHHHHHHHH WRONG!"

No one is more qualified to write what you are writing than you. Just as there is no one with the same fingerprints in the world, there is no one out there with the EXACT same story as you.

My professional speaking clients will tell you I drill into them that they are unique. While the whole world has a wealth of knowledge, everyone drinks from the same well. The difference is, you tell it your way, and I will tell it mine.

Maybe our readers won't relate to me, but they will and can relate to you and what you are saying and doing.

We cannot be everything to everybody. This is why we need you to put your message out there in a way that your loyal followers can understand.

I truly believe in destiny. I believe we have a purpose. I believe your message is meant to be shared.

It isn't about you; it is about the person who needs help solving problems.

If you solve any problem, you have a market. If you solve a problem, you will make money. If you solve a problem, you are doing great things in this world.

Don't let your "inner terrorist" (that little voice in your head sabotaging your dreams) get in the way of achieving the success you so richly deserve.

Chapter Twenty
How to Set Up, Create and Achieve a Mega Successful Book Signing

This is an easy, step-by-step approach to setting up a successful book signing.

It is a great way to gain crucial exposure to sell your books/ workshops, as well as create sales and valuable contacts.

My suggestion is to go on a book tour when you are going on holidays. Keep track of expenses and make sure you book everything at least 6 weeks in advance. This way, you can claim most of your trip as a legitimate business expense (please see your accountant for details).

Another idea to create the perfect book signing tour is to create book signings in and around your own hometown. Make the tour an "around the TOWN" tour... around the town you live in. Then have a look at what you can do within a 3-hour radius. Write those cities down and get to work. Plan for it 6 weeks in advance, one per week (or more if you are ambitious). You will be glad you did.

Be prepared to have speaking material to hand out. Many future speaking programs are grown through book signings in bookstores.

Although bookstores are the traditional route (I will be discussing that later), there are other options as well.

Be creative! Here is a list of possibilities:

1. Malls (without bookstores)
2. Libraries
3. Networking functions
4. Multi-level corporations
5. Churches
6. Associations
7. Pet stores (if they are relevant)
8. Other retail outlets relevant to your subject

Steps for a successful book signing

1. Obtain a list of all the bookstores in the city in which you wish to speak. This would include contact names of managers, addresses, phone numbers, faxes and e-mail addresses. If you possibly can, find out the size of the bookstore and the amount of traffic that flows on any given night. The larger the center, the better.

2. Decide what your program will be: Usually it is a good idea to come with a program. You can do a "reading" or an advice night. You can do a mini-workshop too!

3. Make the calls and ask for the manager. Let him or her know what you have to offer. Usually it is a good idea to come with a program. Tell them you are an author and your book was just released. Ask them if you could possibly do a book signing in their store. Get their name and book the date for which you were hoping.

4. Send a thank you card to the manager: Thank the manager for his or her time, and effort. Let them know they can contact you, if they need ANYTHING prior to the event.

5. Good time to book: Of course you will have to work with the bookstore on this. A general rule of thumb is in the evenings; sometimes Saturday and Sunday are good as well. Ask the manager what date he or she would recommend.

6. Send promotional materials: Let the managers know you will be sending promotional materials. Let them know they can feel free to contact the media. Ask if they would like you to design a promotional flyer they can hand out in their book bags. *A really neat idea is to do up bookmarks or postcards and have them use these.

7. Prepare a consignment agreement: I have attached a sample copy you can use to draft a consignment agreement. Unless you have a TON of stock, don't leave any more than 5 books in the store (prior/after the event). Bring another consignment agreement to use for the day you are there, when you sell more books. Fax this in and get them to sign it as soon as you can.

8. Drop off or mail: Your publicity kit, books, bookmarks, etc., as soon as you have everything set up.

9. Market your own book signing: Send out a press release announcing you are doing a book signing and add a little teaser about what your program for the evening will offer. Send it to ALL media in the area.

10. Marketing Suggestions:
    a) Do a one-page fax out announcing the event.
    b) Tell all your friends in the area.
    c) Send out an e-mail to the list of people you know and ask them to pass it on.
    d) Ask the bookstores to send out a note from you to their client list AND/OR advertise it in their catalogue (get a copy for yourself).
    e) Contact associations or places where your target reader goes and ask them to post/send out an announcement.

11. Arrive about 1 hour early to set up: set up your table with props, water and pens. If you are not at a retail store and you are selling your own books, don't forget to have your own change and order forms.

12. Give the managers a small "announcement" so they can announce to all their patrons 30 minutes, 15 minutes, 5 minutes and 1 minute prior to the event.

13. Prepare another consignment agreement for the evening: Letting the bookstore know you will "take back" extra stock they don't wish you to leave. Use THESE books to walk around the store, introduce yourself and let patrons know you will be doing a book signing. Say: "Here is a copy of my book. Please feel free to browse through it... you can drop it off at my table, if you aren't interested in buying". Then move on to the next. This will develop a rapport and it is fun too!

14. Have a draw box: The name of the game is to get contact names, numbers, etc. Have a draw box so you can e-mail/mail people a note of thanks. This will build your database and that results in future sales!

15. Arrange for a proper introduction: Write up a one-minute "blurb" and NEVER let the person introducing you "wing it". This will help you "lead" your audience to where you want them to go. Mention in here you are available to speak at other events and you would be happy to chat about that after your program.

16. Stand up: Try not to sit down, unless it is an informal setting. Walk around and interact with your audience.

17. GREAT TIP: Read at least one section from your book. Give them a copy to hold on to. Ask them to flip to the page from which you are reading and read along with you. If you do this right, you will boost your sales for the evening. Everyone who markets books knows that if you

get your book into their hands, your chances of those people buying a book will exponentially multiply.

18. GREAT TIP: Always mention a holiday that is coming up and say, "Many of my readers buy two books... one for themselves and one for a friend to give as a gift". Why sell just one when you can sell two or more at a time??

19. When it is over: Make sure you stick around to sign the books and chitchat. You never know what can happen by doing this!

20. Clean up your consignment agreement and the books.

21. Leave autographed copies of your book at the bookstore. Get a sticker that says, "signed by author".

22. Send a thank you note THROUGH the MAIL to the store manager and anyone who helped you at the signing.

23. Send a note to all those who entered your free draw. Perhaps send them a bookmark or something nice. Also send them any marketing material you may have. Don't forget to send the winner an autographed book and any other marketing material you may have.

24. Make sure you keep track: of all the consignment papers, sales you made, how many in the crowd, how many books were sold, etc. This will help you decide if you will be back or if perhaps you need to go to another location.

25. Have fun! That is the most important part of this whole experience!

Then start all over again! Remember, YOU are ultimately the one who will market and sell your books. Small book sales equal larger sales. When you are in the public eye, "anything can happen!"

NOW, LIST ALL THE PLACES YOU WOULD LIKE TO DO A BOOK SIGNING.

REMEMBER THE NON-TRADITIONAL MARKETS TOO!

1. In Canada: McNally Robinson Book Sellers: If you have one in your area and you bought a package with us, we will set this one up for you!

2. Chapters, Indigo, Coles Book Stores...

3. Libraries in your and the surrounding area... Libraries are wonderful for book signings! We have the contact person and will introduce you directly to him/her, if this is something you would like to do. General rule of thumb is you take care of your book sales and give the library a donation of $1 per book AND a copy of your book for their deposit. FABULOUS!

4. Think also, in terms of networking groups, malls, special events, create your own book signings, church groups and associations.

5. Go To Town and Have a Riot! You know the steps you must take to make this a successful event. List below all the book signings you can help create, and PLAN at least 1 per month. It is a great way to get out there.

_____

_____

_____

_____

_____

_____

_____

_____

_____

_____

_____

_____

_____

_____

_____

_____

_____

_____

_____

_____

_____

_____

_____

_____

Chapter Twenty-One
How to Get My Book Listed on Amazon.com

To get your books on Amazon.com you will need your own account. This is a fairly simple process and can be done online.

1. Go to Amazon.com, specifically to the following page: http://www.amazon.com/exec/obidos/subst/partners/direct/direct-application.html/102-7943342-0323325 - this takes you to Amazon.com Advantage Program.

2. Click on and follow the instructions under, "Read more about the Advantage Program". The Advantage program allows you to set up an account and post your book on their website.

3. Note: There are fees so make sure to read all the details, especially those about the annual signup fee, which is $29.95 US, plus their commission procedure. Also check out the "Search Inside the Book" to find out how to use the advanced promotion tools within the program (this includes how to provide them with your cover art and other enhancements). Also remember you will pay all shipping costs to the US.

As with ANY business venture, check everything out BEFORE you decide to move ahead.

Chapter Twenty-Two
How to Get My Book Listed in Chapters (CAN)
How to Set Up Your Own Publishing Company with Chapters

How to Set Up Your Publishing Company with Chapters

1. Call Anne Aversa at 1-905-789-1234 ext 2100.

2. Tell her you are a new publishing company and you would like to know how to get your books into Chapters/Indigo/Coles bookstores.

3. Let her know you would like to know their procedures and process please.

4. Follow her steps.

As with ANY business venture, check everything out BEFORE you decide to move ahead.

Chapter Twenty-Three
How to Get My Book Listed in Barnes & Noble (USA)

How to Set Up Your Publishing Company With Barnes and Noble

1. Go to their website link at: http://www.barnesandno-ble.com/help/cds2.asp?PID=8148&linkid=9&z=y&cds2Pid=9481

2. Become a Vendor of Record.

3. Put together a bibliography of your book(s) and content that will help promote each title.

4. Submit the information with covers and any book reviews you have, including catalogue category (the subject heading under which your book would be catalogued) and more.

5. To submit into the stores directly, you need to submit a copy of the book, along with marketing and promotional plans, any trade reviews, etc. to the following:

The Small Press Department
Barnes & Noble, Inc.
122 Fifth Ave
New York, NY 10011

Everything is on this website is to help you "walk through" the steps. Follow their guidelines and contact them, if you should have any questions.

As with ANY business venture, check everything out BEFORE you decide to move ahead.

Chapter Twenty-Four
How to Get My Books Listed in Private Bookstores

Having your books in bookstores is a great way to get noticed. You do have to be aware that bookstores will take from 30%-55% off the top for their portion of the retail.

There are two ways you can sell to private bookstores:

1. Complete a wholesale contract and a straight agreement (for books bought outright and paid immediately). They will buy a certain number of copies of your book in exchange for wholesale agreements.

2. They will want to place your book on consignment (more on this in the next chapter of this book). Simply put, they will "store your books" in their bookstore and, if they sell, they will give you your percentage. If they don't? They will send them back. Right now, this is the preference for most bookstores. They don't usually want to take the risk unless you are an already proven author in the market.

3. Stores will take the books and pay you wholesale prices WITH the option of returning unsold books and asking for money back on the books that didn't sell.

4. Other non-traditional book markets will buy at wholesale prices without sending unsold books back.

Following are the steps to get your books into privately listed bookstores: (Please see our Canadian Directory for contact information for book buyers across the nation.)

1. Phone the bookstore to see if their customer base would cater to your particular subject.

2. Ask them if you can send them an information package about your new book to see if they would be interested in buying and selling your book.

3. Ask them their policy on consignment or wholesale book orders.

4. They would also like to know what type of marketing you are doing and how you plan to help them sell the books.

5. Follow up. Although this is key to anything you do, it is something you must do to prove your integrity and build great relationships with book buyers.

Chapter Twenty-Five
How to Set Up
Consignment Agreements

This is a typical consignment agreement you can use with bookstores or any other store/venue that have agreed to joint-venture with you to sell your books.

Please make it personalized and professional looking. It is easy to do in a Word format and then convert to PDF for ease of e-mailing.

Putting your book on consignment simply means the vendor (who has a store or a way of selling your books) agrees to do so for a percentage of the sale.

The vendor (bookstore) also agrees to pay you your portion of the sale WHEN the sale is complete. You will need to have them sign an agreement when you leave your books with them.

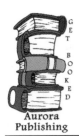

Aurora Publishing

#44 Bernard Way NW,
Calgary, Alberta T3K 2E9
A division of The Opulence Group of Companies Inc.

Phone: 403-230-5946 ext 2
E-mail: aurorapublishing@shaw.ca
Toll Free: 1-877-751-8037

CONSIGNMENT AGREEMENT

GST # 86525 9980 RT0001

Consignment Number: _____ Consignment Date: _____

Partnered With: _____

Address: _____

Phone: _____ FAX: _____ E-mail: _____

Item Description	Retail Price	Quantity	Cost per Unit	Total

Terms and Conditions:
Payment may be via Cheque or Credit Card
All payments should be made to **The Opulence Group of Companies**
Invoice due upon receipt; Shipping will be C.O.D.

GST 7%: _____

Total Due: [   ]

Consignment Agreement:
• Inventory Count Dates: ❏ monthly   ❏ quarterly   ❏ bi-annually
• Terms: _____
_____

• Consignment Discount: _____% Store Signature: _____

Authorized Signature for Aurora Publishing: _____

Chapter Twenty-Six
How to Sell My Initial
100-300 Books NOW!

This process is so exciting! It is a great way to start now - BEFORE you go to print. I also tell my authors to use this platform when they are deciding how many books to print for their first print run.

Really, take some time to put effort into making your list. This is the time for thinking, so make sure you don't have any distractions.

Here are some general guidelines to use:

1) NO "YEAH BUTS"... yeah but, they don't like the type of book I wrote or yeah but he doesn't have any money. PLEASE, just write down the name and let THEM decide for themselves if they wish to buy your book. Nine times out of 10 you will find that they not only buy one copy, they buy two.

2) Remember, people will buy your book just because YOU WROTE IT! Most of these people don't really care what is between the covers... they just care that YOU DID IT! It is really true!

3) Decide that you know 1000 people... BEFORE you go through this exercise. You heard me right, 1000 people - this exercise will be much easier with that mindset.

4) Also write down acquaintances you have met through the people you know when they come to mind. For example, if you know a hairdresser and you have met a friend of hers, then write that friend's name down too.

5) Place more categories in the list than you can think of yourself.

6) If you have someone read you the list while you write it, it may even be easier for you to do this process.

Happy brainstorming ....

1.   Your parents
2.   Your grandparents
3.   Your sisters
4.   Your brothers
5.   Your nieces
6.   Your nephews
7.   Your cousins
8.   Your distant relatives
9.   Your aunts
10. Your uncles
11. Your children
12. Your children's teachers
13. Your teachers from high school
14. Your professors from university
15. Your teachers from college
16. Your friends
17. Your business associates
18. Your clients
19. Your hairdresser
20. Your spouse/partner's relatives
21. Your favourite waiters
22. Your favourite restaurant staff
23. Your favourite liquor store staff
24. Your hairdresser or salon staff
25. Your weight loss group
26. Your networking groups
27. Your rotary clubs
28. Your accountant
29. Your bookkeeper
30. Your chamber of commerce

31. Your old address book
32. Your e-mail list
33. Your clients' e-mail lists (joint ventures)
34. Your classmates from school
35. Your classmates from college or university
36. Your classmates in personal development courses
37. Your classmates in continuing education courses
38. Your old work partners at your job
39. People you work with currently
40. People at your work
41. Managers you know, old and current
42. Sports coaches
43. Gym patrons and staff
44. Grocery store clerks and staff
at   Your local grocery store
45. Mall bookstore owners you know
46. Retail owners and staff
47. Librarians
48. Fast food places you frequent
49. Dentist and staff
50. Orthodontists and staff
51. Doctors and their staff
52. Massage therapists
53. People who do Reiki
54. Dance instructors
55. Parents of your children's friends
56. Vet and staff
57. Delivery drivers
58. Mechanics
59. Church groups
60. Chiropractor
61. Your bank and staff
62. Your mentors
63. Acupuncturists
64. Your eye doctor
65. Your paper carrier
66. Your lawyer
67. Starbucks or other local coffee shops' staff
68. Staff of donut shops

69. Receptionists at your suppliers
70. Your office supply store and staff
71. Video rentals and staff
72. Drugstore and staff
73. Your spouse's/significant others' friends
74. Co-workers
75. Clients
76. Doctors
77. Acquaintances
78. Photographer
79. Party-Lite Candles
80. Amway
81. Picture organizers
82. Legacy for Life
83. Herbal Life
84. Melaleuca
85. Tropical Interiors
86. Daycare
87. Babysitters
88. Computer whiz
89. Travel agent and staff
90. Authors
91. Avon reps
92. Regal reps
93. Nikken
94. Internet provider and staff
95. Web page designer
96. Creative Memories
97. Excel
98. Other long distance companies
99. Advertising companies
100. People who produce newsletters, etc.
101. Other multi-level marketing companies
102. Your target markets associations.

103. _____

104. _____

105. _____

106. _____

107. _____

108. _____

109. _____

110. _____

111. _____

112. _____

113. _____

114. _____

115. _____

116. _____

117. _____

118. _____

119. _____

120. _____

121. _____

122. _____

123. _____

124. _____

Chapter Twenty-Seven
A Marketing Miracle, Making Money on Your Books BEFORE You Have Them in Your Hands

This concept is the easiest to understand but very few authors take advantage of its power. I used this with my very first book, *Breaking Through Your Business Barriers!* And as a result sold over 80,000 copies in its first year without it ever being in my hands!

I can't tell you what a wonderful thing it was to have that many copies sold and help me with my publishing and printing costs.

The technique I used? PRE-SELL copies!

Simply put: showing associations, your client base, your friends, your neighbours, etc., a "copy" of what they will get in their book and asking if they would buy now, in order to get a "deal" on the subject. I also am using this technique to pre-sell copies of this book.

7 Steps You Can Take Right Now to Pre-Sell Your Book Effortlessly

1. Create a sales letter telling your readers how you will solve their problems for them.

2. Set up a website with the sales letter attached and set it up to accept payment right online.

3. Make it a benefit to your buyer to buy your "publisher's advance copy" now instead of waiting until it is in the bookstores.

- You could give a discount: "It will be $19.95 plus tax in the bookstores OR you can buy it from me now for only $15.95!"

- You could tell them they will get special reports or free e-books or any other items you can pull together that would be of interest to your buyers if they order now.

4. Start to drive traffic to your website.

5. Send out your sales letters to others who have the same client base as you do, find associations that stand to benefit by having your book presented to their clients.

6. Go to the press and start to send out press releases... this is the time to get moving on your book sales! It is PRIME TIME. Don't miss out on it.

7. Go to bookstores, if it is a HOT topic, and see if they would like to buy. I did this and had several bookstores wanting to place their order right away.

This is the time to get moving on your book sales! It is PRIME TIME. Don't miss out on it.

What are the benefits of pre-sales?

Well, the number one reason is to help balance the cost of self-publishing. It is also a great way to make your bank account soar. I have had several authors use this technique to make anywhere from $20 to tens of thousands of dollars.

The downside? If you don't deliver and finish your book when you say you will, it becomes very dicey. There can always be delays. If you are honest with your buyers, then this process shouldn't be difficult.

You decide, and whatever you choose, just GO FOR IT!

Chapter Twenty-Eight
Non-Traditional Markets
to EXPLODE Sales

I love these ideas! See if this list will help prompt even MORE ideas in your portfolio of marketing and bookselling.

Why are non-traditional book signings more lucrative than traditional bookstore book signings?

The obvious is easy, because bookstores, as we have already discussed, can ask for a large percentage of the retail price to sell in their store. From 30-55% can be a big stretch if you have done a small print run (less than 500 books) for your first release.

I still think it is important to have a book signing in a large store or have your books placed in a large chain or book-store because it will lend you a huge amount of credibility.

With non-traditional book signings, you will be able to keep most, if not all, the money you make. That adds up if you are feeding your moneymaking business funnel.

1. **Library.** Follow the same guidelines we used for the book signings. Find the "friends of the library" to help you promote your book signings. Chat with them and have ample time for everyone to pull their customers in.

Think about it? How many libraries do you have in your area alone? How many in your province/state? How many across the nation?

I would also suggest you simply offer a copy to the library as a small gesture of good faith. They don't ask for anything in return, but giving 10% would be a very nice gesture and the library would be willing to help you out even more.

If you have one book signing per week and sell only 10 books at each, this equals 520 books in a year!

A library tour is an exciting way to practice your book signing and to make sales. Posters will drive people to your website too. Please, really think about this option.

2. **Tradeshows:** Sell your books right at the table. But what is most important is gathering names through draws, etc. Send out invitations to book signings or to visit your website. Your database is what you need to build to make your business a booming success.

3. **Place your book on Amazon.com** and other online book stores. The wave of the future is buying online. The companies who sell online know who will buy certain books, for example, Stephen King novels. Then they go to Stephen King and say, "we will give you two million dollars to send us a special edition novel that you won't sell to anyone else". This will be a Limited Edition. They can make the price of the book higher in order to sell them as a collector's item. Then they e-mail out this offer to their clients and watch the millions grow.

Amazon will help you build your book to a number one bestseller. There are many things you can do if you are affiliated with them. Ask how they can help you become a number one bestseller and see what it is they give you.

They are the largest bookstore in the world. Don't miss out.

4. **Networking Groups:** They love authors, and if you speak for free, you can sell your books as back-end. I went to a networking group and sold over 50 books in 20 minutes when I was selling my book: *101 Tips to Become a Networking Genius.*

You never know when you start this journey how this will expand and get you going in a direction you will love.

5. **Speak at your own events:** RIGHT, have your own book signing. Give a keynote for free OR start a workshop and sell tickets with your book as back-end.

6. **Speaking to other groups:** help wanted groups, church groups, associations, etc.

7. **Distributors:** They have built in clients. They, for example multi-level marketing companies and corporations, will buy wholesale.

8. **Joint venture** with others who have an e-mail list. They get a percentage of the sales and you get the money right off the bat. I love joint ventures. It helps so many people at one time.

9. **Ask your clients for referrals:** This really works. Word of mouth is a great way to add to your client base and increase your income.

10. **Direct Mail Marketing:** This is a fabulous way of creating more sales. I used a short sales letter and sent it out to teachers, pastors and coaches to draw them to my website.

We had some great success because not only do I have my book on my website but I have a great deal more in depth sales letter. I also have a package to help authors get their books out in a less expensive, more time efficient, high quality way.

This is of great advantage to make "higher sales" for less upfront costs.

You should find a mentor who has had huge success with direct mail marketing. They know how to set up the copy sales letter to dramatically increase sales.

Take action today. You created your book for a reason. Don't sit on them, letting the pages rot in place. Sell them! Enjoy them! Pass around the goodness that comes from your effort.

Claim your own copy of:

Libraries Across Canada Directory

Contact information for libraries across our nation so that you can set up a book signing tour across Canada and soar!

www.howtowriteandpublish.com

Retail: $49.00

CHAPTER TWENTY-NINE
ATTRACTING THE PRESS

What you need to do to gain exposure with the media.

WHY WOULD I WANT FREE PUBLICITY?

This is a great piece to the puzzle and a great deal of fun. If you need help writing a press release, we do offer a home-study course. It is available at www.kathleenmailer.com under "Get the Press".

You will want to get publicity because:

1. Gives you HUGE credibility.

2. Helps you reach TONS of people in a short period of time.

3. VERY cost effective; cost is next to nothing.

4. It helps you reach a more "targeted" market.

AND SO MANY MORE REASONS!

Send out a press release every time you are doing a book signing or event. It will help you explode your sales in the next 12 months.

PRESS KIT FOR A BOOK

What you should include in your press kit

A great rule of thumb is to buy a folder with an insert pocket on each side. This is called a presentation folder. This will show off your press kit well.

Stagger the edges so you can easily see the "titles" of each section. This may take a bit of work but it is worth it.

The kit will look like this:

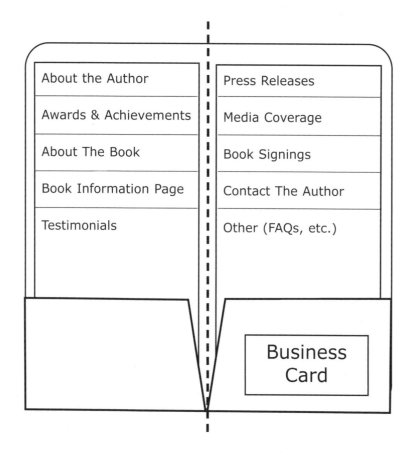

About the Author	Press Releases
Awards & Achievements	Media Coverage
About The Book	Book Signings
Book Information Page	Contact The Author
Testimonials	Other (FAQs, etc.)

Business Card

- You already have the <u>About the Author</u> page.

- You already know how to get your <u>Press Releases</u>.

- <u>Awards & Achievements</u>, list all the things of which you are proud and all your accomplishments.

- <u>About the Book</u> - Book information page - you have already done this in the package.

- List of all <u>Media Coverage</u>.

- List of <u>Book Signings</u> already done or an invitation to one you are in the process of doing.

" <u>Contact the Author</u> - Contact information page.

Good luck! And Enjoy!

KATHLEEN D. MAILER

The Coach's Coach

Kathleen is renowned for her energy, enthusiasm and drive to make a difference in the world. Her growing list of accomplishments have made her a sought-out speaker for conference planners and event coordinators alike. A self-made woman, she is President of Aurora Publishing, has authored several books, is a talented Coach and Speaker and is Dean of The Opulence Academy. She meets with both individuals and groups to assist them in recognizing the opportunities that exist and provides the tools necessary to make them work.

Contact information:

Kathleen D. Mailer
#354-300-8120 Beddington Blvd. NW
Calgary, Alberta T3K 2A8
403-230-5946 ext 3
mastersmentor@shaw.ca

www.howtowriteandpublish.com
www.kathleenmailer.com
www.yourchoicebooks.info

AUTHOR - MOTIVATIONAL SPEAKER - MENTOR - ENTREPRENEUR

BOOKS BY KATHLEEN MAILER

Why we like it: We love it because it is filled with peoples' dreams come true. Talent of often first-time writers showcasing their genius! It is a quick, inspirational read. It showcases a wonderful array of talent - from an 11 year-old student, to an electrician, to life coaches.

Who will love it: Anyone who wants a dose of inspiration or a reminder that dreams do come true. A quote a day will keep the blues away and this book definitely does that! OR, someone who loves the "Chicken Soup" books; equally motivating and sincere.

Here are a few words from the compiler of the stories: Kathleen D. Mailer:

In all my years of coaching, I have come to understand the depth of the untapped gifts we have that are just waiting to be discovered. These gifts often lay dormant deep in our souls until they are gently coaxed out by someone who recognizes the light that burns with a desire to change the world.

I liken these brilliant people to the finest orange trees in all the land. Their contributions bring forth the sweetest, juciest, most mouth-watering fruit. Wouldn't we all want to sample this fruit? The tragedy is we don't recognize our ability in ourselves, so the untapped resources of life-giving inspiration, motivation and thought are never manifested for the world to rejoice.

The authors in this book are breaking free from their shells. They are sharing their luminosity and changing their world, one page at a time.

This book is for you. It is for me. It is for the writer and his/her new found freedom.

COLLECTIVE SOUL™ SERIES - VOLUME ONE

Books by Kathleen Mailer

Why we like it: We love it because we found a genuine meat and potatoes approach to business-building. It is all there - set up of your office, hot marketing strategies, profit-cultivating ideas, business plans, increasing your credibility, how to acquire funding, networking, team building, goal setting, database building, and so much more!

Who will love it: Anyone who is a business owner or a team builder who wants to bypass the barriers that one faces when building her/his business. OR someone who loved the books, *Small Business Marketing for Dummies* ™ by Barbara Findley Schenck; *Dig Your Well Before You're Thirsty: The Only Networking Book You'll Ever Need* by Harvey Mackay, or any other dynamic business book that entails an all-inclusive look of aspects of your small or home-based business.

Here are a few words about *Breaking Through Your Business Barriers* from well-respected business leaders and book reviewers:

AWE-some listed books offering valuable information for women in business. Kathleen... has taken what seems to be the most dramatic barriers to a home-based or small business and broken them up into manageable pieces. This book addresses barriers such as: how to start, money issues, business recognition, propelling your business forward and creating balance.

AWEIA - Alberta Women's Enterprise Initiative Association

Kathleen teaches leadership and networking skills in her dynamic training seminars. Each boasts a wealth of information... she has compiled her knowledge and information [in] "Breaking Throught Your Business Barriers."

Paula Steele, Business Dynamics Magazine

Breaking Through Your Business Barriers - 3rd edition

Booкs by Kathleen Mailer

Take a daily walk through a magnificent rock garden of Ms. Mailer's own design. With each step you will transform your thoughts so that you can manifest a life filled with excrutiating joy, overflowing abundance, satisfying and fulfilling rela-tionships, passionate purpose and burning desire to be somebody and do something huge with your life. Awaken your soul to the spiritual lessons from The ROCK.

Mailer is the next Laurie Beth Jones (author of "Jesus CEO" and "Jesus in Blue Jeans"). Her daily inspiration will breathe the characteristics of a spiritual genius into your life, helping you to convert your negative perceptions (which have held your head under water while you are drowning) into a profound and highly impacting life.

Kimberley Langford, Editor
Insight News Magazine

"Lessons From the ROCK" feeds my soul.

Raymond Aaron, co-author
Chicken Soup for the Canadian Parent's Soul

Leadership Wisdom from the ROCK

WHAT PEOPLE ARE SAYING

When I bring Kathleen in to speak to a group of our clients, it is like opening up a can of "Whoop-A*S"! She wows them with her energy, and motivates them to move mountains with her business.

Robin Morrison, Calgary, Alberta
Events Coordinator
Above Average Entrepreneur Conference

Kathleen's a positive and powerful entrepreneur dedicated to passing on her knowledge to others. She has a razor-sharp ability to create and achieve enormous goals. I have personally seen the dramatic improvement in people's lives, careers and income just by learning from Kathleen.

Raymond Aaron, Toronto, Ontario
Monthly Mentor Program, Nation's Business Coach,
Co-author *Chicken Soup for the Canadian Parent's Soul,*
Canada's Who's Who for helping to make the most
CANADIAN millionaires in real estate

Kathleen's brings a spark and enthusiasm to any speaking event! She obviously cares deeply about her audience and motivates them to take action. Her talks are packed with honesty, straightforwardness and no-hold-barred energy. Have Kathleen wake up and get any person going in the right direction.

Kay Ballard, Vancouver, BC
Stategic Mentor
Magic of Wealth Seminars

ABOUT KATHLEEN MAILER

WORKƒHOPƒ AND HOME ƒTUDY

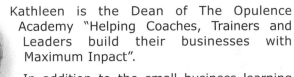

Kathleen is the Dean of The Opulence Academy "Helping Coaches, Trainers and Leaders build their businesses with Maximum Inpact".

In addition to the small business learning opportunities, Kathleen delivers workshops around the world to provide people with the tools they need to achieve their dreams.

Manifest Your Dreams! - helps coaches, leaders and trainers develop their own businesses so that they can enjoy immediate, mid-term and long-term profits! They can leave a legacy!

How to Write & Publish Your OWN Book: From Conception to Bookstore in 90 Days! - a workshop which delivers results.

Deluxe Publishing Package - allows want-to-be authors to *become* authors in a short time frame. You can make money writing RIGHT NOW!

Leadership Wisdom™Series - a 14 month coaching program that helps coaches, trainers and leaders build their businesses with MAXIMUM IMPACT! Correspondence Program.

Heart Talks Boot Camp - designed to help those "who want to BE somebody and DO something with their life" in terms of creating and writing their own book and self-help programs within 6 to 8 weeks. Includes physical book finished, published and signed by the author at his/her very own book signing.

The Prosperity Matrix™Series - a 12 month coaching program that helps you change your thoughts and mindset from one of poverty to that of prosperity.

Who's in Charge of Your Destiny? You or Your Inner Terrorist? - answers the age-old questions: "What am I supposed to do with my life?" and "Why do I hold myself back?"

PROGRAMƒ BY KATHLEEN MAILER

Awards and Achievements

2004...
- **Designed workshop "Manifest Your Dreams!** to help coaches, trainers and leaders develop their own businesses so they can enjoy immediate, short-term and long-term profits. They can leave a legacy!
- **Published the Collective Soul™Series - Limited Edition**

- **Created Deluxe Publishing Package** - allows want-to-be authors to *become* authors in a short time frame. You can make money writing RIGHT NOW!

- **Designed How to Write & Publish Your OWN Book: From Conception to Bookstore in 90 Days!** - a workshop which delivers results.

2003...

- **Designed Leadership Wisdom™Series** - a 14 month coaching program that helps coaches, trainers and leaders build their businesses with MAXIMUM IMPACT!

- **Published the Canadian Small Biz Almanac** - to help small business owners create credibility and marketing material for their businesses.

- **Leadership Wisdom from the ROCK: Transform Your Thoughts, Manifest Your Dreams** - will impart courage, inspiration and resolution to the everyday moments in your life. It is for those of you who are ready, willing and able to make monumental changes from the inside out through daily meditations, thoughts and actions.

- **Heart Talks Boot Camp** - designed to help those "who want to BE somebody and DO something with their life" in terms of creating and writing their own book and self-help programs within 6 to 8 weeks. Includes physical book finished, published and signed by the author at his/her very own book signing.

AWARDS AND ACHIEVEMENTS

2002...

- **Inspirational Thoughts for Wavemakers of the World!** - an audio book designed to inspire you to impact positively on the world around you.

2001...

- **Your Journey to Passion - Uncover Your Destiny** - this audio book helps YOU to be all you were meant to be.

2000...

- **Designed The Prosperity Matrix™Series** - a 12 month coaching program that helps you change your thoughts and mindset from one of poverty to that of prosperity.

- **Dean of The Opulence Academy for Small and Home Business** - our correspondence school was designed to build Leaders in Prosperity.

1999...

- **Breaking Through Your Business Barriers!** - an **Entrepreneurial Handbook for Small and Home Business.**

- **Entrepreneur Hall of Fame** - Monthly Mentor Program (a group of over 600 entrepreneurs). This special award is given for the extraordinary achievements, dedication and self-education so significant that you have fulfilled the very high standards required to win Entrepreneur of the Year and/or Player of the Year more than once.

- **Player of the Year** - in honour of your demonstration of the true entrepreneurial spirit, The Raymond Aaron Group hereby recognizes your considerable accomplishments towards your own Life Goals, in addition to your open-hearted willingness to give to others.

KATHLEEN MAILER

AWARDΓ AND ACHIEVEMENTΓ

- **1999 Wall of Recognition** - The Best in Business Awards, Saber TEC/Business Dynamics - she has always gone out of her way to "serve" other people and help them in any way she can. She is very credible, and stands behind her word, no matter what. When she says something is done, it is done.

- **Nominated for Best in Professional Integrity Award**

- **Nominated for the Best in Sheer Enthusiasm Award - Best in Business Awards**

- **Nominated for Entrepreneur of the Year Award** - Calgary Chamber of Commerce

1998...

- **Entrepreneur of the Year Award** - Entrepreneur Program, Monthly Mentor

- **Player of the Year Award** - Entrepreneur Program, Monthly Mentor

1997...

- **Entrepreneur of the Year Award** - Entrepreneur Program, Monthly Mentor

1996...

- **Entrepreneur of the Year Award** - Entrepreneur Program, Monthly Mentor

SECTION FIVE:

I AM OVERWHELMED, IS THERE AN EASIER WAY?

CHAPTER THIRTY
LET'S REVIEW

There is a great deal to think about - that I can agree with!

Let's go through a review of what you need and the costs associated with your needs.

1. **Cover Design & Layout Specialist** - You need someone who knows what he or she is doing and has experience in the industry. He/She must have the right program and will do not only the cover but also will do the layout. Two costs are covered in the pricing below:

Average range of costs associated with this project: **$1000.00-$3500.00.**

2. **Editing** - Depending upon the length of your manuscript and the duties you want your editor to perform, your editing costs can become a very substantial investment. It is WORTH the investment though.

Average range of costs associated with this project: **$45-$100/hr.**

3. **Marketing Materials** - Again, each project is different. It depends what it is you are looking for. Postcards, posters, business cards and bookmarks can cost the price of layout and design as well as printing.

Average range of costs associated with this project: **$500.00-$1500.00.**

4. **PR person** - To create and send out your press release to media venues across the nation. This cost truly depends upon the individual company.

Average range of costs associated with this project: **$750.00-$20,0000.00.**

5. **Illustrations or Artist for Children's Books**: If you are a children's author or an author in need of illustrations in your book, this investment could be substantial as well.

Average range of costs associated with this project: **$750.00-$10,000.000.**

6. **Barcode production for the ISBN number** - As I mentioned in this book, you have to have this done in a certain program.

Average range of costs associated with this project: **$50.00-$75.00.**

Remember to take into consideration the time frame for gathering a team and working on your book. There is also marketing time involved and the best one to market your book is YOU.

So, how much is your time worth? That is the question you will want to ask yourself.

Can I do it any cheaper with the same quality?

I just want my book to be done.

YES! Let our experienced team help you. We actually have a package that is all-inclusive.

We know time is money and in this industry it helps to have someone guide you and walk you through each step.

It becomes effortless to achieve such an amazing goal so quickly.

At the moment, this is what we are offering our family of authors. (*Please contact our office for more details, as we may have changed our package policy. OR view our website for more details. www.howtowriteandpublish.com)

The cost is minimal and less than what it usually costs for cover design alone.

Here is what you get:

You receive a **30 minute consultation** to discover:

a   What your book will be about.
b   Pricing your book.
c   Complete outline of your book so you can write it in record-breaking time.
d   A "choose-to-do list" of exactly what you must do in order to get your ISBN number and your cover design done.

Coupon & Directory of Editors who will supply you with an hourly fee of $15/hr for this project AND a FREE estimate. Plus a Special Report: How to Find the Perfect Editor *This is a matching service provided by Aurora Publishing. We are in NO way endorsing any or all editors. As with any business, please follow proper business procedures.

Professional Cover Design and Layout of Your Book- so that you can get it printer-ready & increase your sales because **we DO judge a book by its cover!**

Your book formatted as an eBook so that you can sell it electronically on your Web site or other Web sites and make residual income from your book.

To Ghost Write or NOT to Ghost Write - THIS IS THE QUESTION We will supply you with our Ghost Write Directory of ghost writers who have agreed to a special Ghost Writer's Coupon for those who have received this package.*This is a matching service provided by Aurora Publishing. We are in NO way endorsing any or all ghost writers. As with any business, please follow proper business procedures.

Get Listed on Our On-Line Bookstore We will NOT take a fee for this service at this time; your orders will come directly to you! (Soon to be Released!) www.yourchoice-books.info

Children's Book Illustrator: We will supply you with our directory of Children's Book Illustrators who have agreed to special Coupons for those who have received this package. *This is a matching service provided by Aurora Publishing. We are in NO way endorsing any or all illustrators. As with any business, please follow proper business procedures.

Special Report: **10 Sizzling Ideas to Make You Even More Money Writing!**

<u>Special Report</u>: **7 Steps to Show You How to Tap into the Most FANTASTIC Markets that Pay YOU to Write for them.**

<u>Directory</u>: 150+ Magazine Contacts In Order to Sell Your Articles and Create A Buzz for your Book.

<u>Get the Press for Authors!</u> - At Home Study Workshop/ Workbook/Video to help you get the publicity you deserve! Here is what is in the package. $349.00 Value

a   Instant Credibility: Your One-Page Marketing Miracle that you will use for every piece of marketing now and in the future

b   The Press Kit: Components and Information Media Will Want to Review

c   Working Through the Press Release

d   How to Get $1 Million Dollars Worth of Free Publicity VIDEO - by PR GURU.... Paul Hartunian

e   Book Review: In our magazine: The Networker News - (*subject to change without notice) NOTE: How much is a full-page write-up/review worth if you were to buy it as advertising?

f   COMES COMPLETE WITH EXAMPLES FOR REVIEW.

More information at: www.howtowriteandpublish.com

Section Six:

What Are Some Other Ways of Selling My Writing?

Chapter Thirty-One
How to Write Articles & Pitch Them to Magazines

Writing the Article

1. Decide on your subject for the article. Remember, if you solve a problem for someone he/she will love you forever.

2. Create your title. Make it eye-catching.

3. Create an introductory paragraph.

4. List 7 tips, tricks or techniques to help your readers understand that their problem IS solvable.

5. Recap in your closing paragraph.

6. List a "tag line", so that readers know you are the expert and also the author of... with a website for contact information.

Tips to getting your article placed:

1. Find the magazines you wish to submit to/write for.

2. Contact them and ask for writer's guidelines and preferred word count.

3. Find out the theme their publication is presenting in the months to come and write your article to fit that theme.

4. Follow the guidelines to the letter.

In section 7 of this book there is a partial directory of magazines you can contact to receive their information on submitting articles.

Go make some money!!!

JUST A NOTE: if you remember what I said, you can also write and have your articles published with no cash exchanging hands. It is a great way to get publicity and drive people to your website. Don't miss the opportunity for exposure!!

Chapter Thirty-Two
Become a Ghostwriter

I have done some research on this subject and there is money in ghostwriting.

If you are someone who loves to research and write essays and reports, then you may want to submit your work to www.elance.com or put your name in our ghostwriter directory.

Contact us for more information.

Ghostwriters have been known to make $250-$75,000 plus depending upon his/her experience and clientele.

Chapter Thirty-Three

Become a Copywriter

Copywriters make money! Everyone is looking for sales copy for back cover copy design for their books, sales letters, websites and the like.

If you have a knack and you want some more know-how? Please do get some copywriting experience and courses.

If you are good at this, you will have a steady stream of people banging down your door begging you to please work for them.

A good copywriter makes anywhere from $500.00-$100,000.00, depending upon his/her experience and clientele.

CHAPTER THIRTY-FOUR
BECOME A COLUMNIST

Just like an article journalist or free-lancer, becoming a columnist can be lucrative as well. Look for publications that "fit" with your experience.

Being an author definitely lends credibility to your portfolio and becoming a columnist can generate great leads to sell books.

Think about it. Can you take bits and pieces of your book and cut and paste into a column "sampling" every week or month? Of course you can!

Go baby go!

SECTION SEVEN:

BONUS:
MILLION DOLLAR
DIRECTORY AT
YOUR FINGERTIPS

Chapter Thirty-Five
Bookstores & Book Buyers Across Canada

To see a list of over 1500 bookstores and book buyers across Canada, please go to:

http://www.howtowriteandpublish.com/index_files/cbook-stores.html

The list is just too large to reproduce here.

** Our directories are as up-to-date as possible. We will not guarantee exact contact information is completely correct. Please use the Internet to upgrade any material that is out of date. Thank you.

CHAPTER THIRTY-SIX
LIBRARIES OF THE WORLD

List of main libraries and their contact information for around the world.

National Library of Canada:
http://nlc-bnc.ca
395 Wellington Street, Ottawa, Ontario K1A 0N4
(613) 996-1623
Telephone: (613) 995-9481 or 1-877-896-9481
(Toll free in Canada)
TDD: (613) 992-6969 or 1-866-299-1699
(Toll free in Canada)
Fax: (613) 943-1112
On-line Reference Enquiry Form at:
www.nlc-bnc.ca/6/1/s1-700-e.html

United States National Libraries
http://www.libdex.com/country/USA.html

National Library of Australia.
http://www.nla.gov.au

Biblioteca Nacional.
http://www.bn.br

National Library of China.
http://nlc.nlc.gov.cn

Biblioteca Nacional de Colombia.
http://www.presidencia.gov.co

Bibliothèque nationale de France. French National Library.
http://www.bnf.fr

Die Deutsche Bibliothek. The National Library of Germany.
http://www.ddb.de

Országos Széchényi Könyvtár (OSZK).
National Széchényi Library.
http://www.oszk.hu

Library of Iceland.
http://www.bok.hi.is

Biblioteca Nazionale Centrale di Firenze.
The Central National Library of Florence.
http://www.bncf.firenze.sbn.it

National Diet Library.
http://www.ndl.go.jp/index-e.html

Biblioteca Nacional de Mexico.
http://biblional.bibliog.unam.mx/bib01.html

National Library of Scotland
http://www.nls.uk

Biblioteca Nacional. National Library of Spain.
http://www.bne.es

Kungliga Biblioteket. The Royal Library.
http://www.kb.se

Schweizerische Landesbibliothek.
Bibliothèque Nationale Suisse. National Library of Switzerland.
http://www.snl.ch

Millî Kütüphane. National Library of Turkey.
http://www.mkutup.gov.tr

Llyfrgell Genedlaethol Cymru. National Library of Wales.
http://www.llgc.org.uk

Chapter Thirty-Seven
Book Fairs and Festivals to Sell Your Book

Book Fairs are a great place to sell your book or to get picked up by a big publisher.

APA Australian Book Fair
http://www.bookfair.com.au/index.asp

Baltimore Book Festival
http://www.bop.org/calendar/events/book_index.html

BookExpo America (BEA), Chicago
http://www.bookexpoamerica.com/App/homepage.cfm?moduleid=42&appname=288

BookExpo Canada, Toronto
http://www.reedexpo.ca/bookexpo

BookWorld, Prague
http://www.bookworld.cz

Border Book Festival, Las Cruces, New Mexico
http://www.zianet.com/bbf

Boston International Antiquarian Book Fair
http://www.bostonbookfair.com

Buckeye Book Fair, Wooster, Ohio
http://www.the-dailyrecord.com/ past_issues/bookfair/bookfair_index.html

Cairo International Book Fair
http://www.cibf.org/en/index.cfm

California International Antiquarian Book Fair, San Francisco
http://www.sanfranciscobookfair.com

Central Coast Book and Author Festival, San Luis Obispo, CA
http://www.ccbookfest.org

Connecticut Children's Book Fair
http://bookfair.uconn.edu

Florida Antiquarian Booksellers Association
http://floridabooksellers.com/bookfair.html

Frankfurt Book Fair, Germany
http://www.frankfurt-bookfair.com/en/portal.html

Georgia Antiquarian Book Fair, Georgia
http://www.gaba.net/bookfair.htm

Hong Kong Book Fair
http://hkbookfair.tdc.org.hk

Leftwords Festival of Books & Ideas, Toronto, Canada
http://www.web.net/~leftword

London International Bookfair
http://www.libf.co.uk

Long Island Antiquarian Fall Book Fair
http://liabda.com/bookfair.htm

Mid-Atlantic Literary Small Press Conference and
Book Fair, Maryland
http://www.writer.org/bookfair

New York Antiquarian Book Fair
http://www.abaa.org/pages/nybf.html

Northwest Bookfest, Seattle, Washington
http://www.nwbookfest.org

Ottawa Small Press Book Fair
http://www.track0.com/rob_mclennan/small_press_book_
fair.htm

Seattle Antiquarian Book Fair
http://www.seattlebookfair.com/index.htm

Small Press Book Fair, New York
http://www.smallpress.org/bookfair/bookfair.htm

South Carolina Book Festival & Antiquarian Book Fair
http://www.schumanities.org/bookfestival.htm

Tokyo International Book Fair
http://web.reedexpo.co.jp/tibf/english

Vilnius Book Fair, Lithuania
http://www.elnet.lt/business/02-01/02.htm

Washington Antiquarian Book Fair
http://www.wabf.com

York National Book Fair, England
http://www.yorkbookfair.com

Chapter Thirty-Eight
Publishers

Comprehensive list of book publishers and their requirements should you decide to take your next print run to the publisher.

A.B.L.E., Inc.
http://www.angelicbeingsoflight.com
Atlanta, Georgia, United States

Description:

Titles include:
1) The true story of the author/publisher's personal experience in completely healing a "chronic and incurable" illness.
2) An inspiring and helpful workbook for others to heal themselves.
3) A CD of a guided meditation for healing and problem resolution.

Formats:
Audio, Books

Topics:
New Age, Personal Growth, Self-Help, Spirituality

Contact Information:
Angelic Beings of Light
Lois M. Grant, Ph.D.
404.252.8525 tel.
404.252.3441 fax

A.M. Best Company
http://www.ambest.com
Oldwick, New Jersey, United States

Description:
"A.M. Best Company, The Insurance Information Source, offers comprehensive, quality data to insurance professionals."

Formats:
Books, Software

Topics:
Business & Commerce, Reference

Contact Information:
Global Headquarters
A.M. Best Company, Inc.
Ambest Road
Oldwick, NJ 08858
(908) 439-2200

Corporate Offices

1. A.M. Best Europe
11th Floor, 1 Minster Court
Mincing Lane
London, England EC3R 7AA
Telephone:+44 (0)20 7626 6264

2. A.M. Best Asia-Pacific Ltd.
Unit 5707, 57/F Central Plaza
18 Harbour Rd.
Wanchai, Hong Kong
852-2827-3400

Aardwolfe Books
http://www.aardwolfe.com
Hawaii, United States

Description:
Fiction publisher of historical novels on the Middle-East, Islam, Muslim culture & history, and the Caliphate. Book seller. Accepting manuscripts.

Recent title:
Khalifah by John Elray.

Formats:
Books, E-Books

Topics:
Archaeology & Anthropology, Fiction, History, Literature, Religion/Other

Contact Information:
Aardwolfe Books
PO Box 471
Aiea, HI 96701-0471
publisher@aardwolfe.com

Abbeville Press
http://www.abbeville.com
New York, New York, United States

Description:
"An international publisher and distributor of art and illustrated books, as well as stationery and printed gift items. Its headquarters are in New York, with offices in Paris

Formats:
Books

Topics:
Art & Architecture, Children's Books, Food, Photography

ABC Feelings, Inc./Adage
http://www.abcfeelings.com
Hayden Lake, Idaho, United States

Description:
Feelings awareness and communication publications and other character development tools for children and those who work with them.

Formats:
Audio, Booklets, Books, Games, Manuals, Online Information, Newsletters, Posters

Topics:
Childcare/Parenting, Children's Books, Education, Personal Growth, Psycholog

Contact Information:
info@abcfeelings.com

Active Parenting Publishers
http://www.activeparenting.com
Kennesaw, Georgia, United States

Description:
Videos, books and online classes for helping you raise courageous, responsible children.

Formats:
Audio, Booklets, Books, Film/Video, Games, Multimedia CDs, Online Information, Posters

Topics:
Childcare/Parenting, Families

Contact Information:
Active Parenting USA
Headquarters:
1955 Vaughn Rd. NW, Suite 108
Kennesaw, GA 30144-7808
Phone: 770-429-0565
Toll-Free: 800-825-0060 or
800-235-7755
Fax: 770-429-0334
E-mail: cservice@activeparenting.com

ACU Press - Abilene Christian University
http://www.acu.edu/campusoffices/acupress
Abilene, Texas, United States

Formats:
Audio, Books

Topics:
Religion/Christian

Contact Information:
ACU Press
Abilene Christian University
ACU Station Box 29138
Abilene, Texas 79699
1-800-444-4228 or (325) 674-2720
8:00 am - 5:00 pm CST, Monday-Friday
FAX: 325-674-6471
e-mail: jean.cook@acu.edu

Adams Business Media
http://www.abm.net
Arlington Heights, Illinois, United States

Description:
"Focus is on developing, acquiring and operating business to business publications, industry websites, industry book and video sales, data mining, custom publishing and multimedia marketing projects for key, growth-oriented markets."

Formats:
Magazines

Topics:
Business & Commerce

Contact Information:
Chicago
833 West Jackson, 7th Floor
Chicago, IL 60607
Phone: 312-846-4600
Fax: 312-977-1042

Connecticut
17 High Street, 2nd Floor
Norwalk, CT 06851
ph 203-855-8499
fx 203-855-9446

Palm Springs
420 S. Palm Canyon Dr. 2nd Flr
Palm Springs, CA 92262
ph 760-318-7000
fx 760-323-4877

Sonoma
Buyside Magazine
200 Siesta Way, Ste. 200
Sonoma, CA 95476

ph 707-933-2800
fx 707-933-2820

Sonoma
JQ Magazine
585 5th Street
Sonoma, CA 95476
ph 707-938-1082
fx 707-938-6585

New York
304 Park Ave S. 11th Floor
New York, NY 10010
Darcey 212-590-2475
Heather 212-590-2477
fx 212.590.2476

San Francisco
585 Howard St. 2nd Floor
San Francisco, CA 94105
ph 415-621-0220
fx 415-348-0222

Ant Hill Press
http://www.connectforjobs.org/jobfeed/web/LogonPage.jsp
Sandwich, Massachusetts, United States

Description:
"A small press dedicated to "charting old wisdom and dis-
covering new possibilities." We offer inspirational pathways
to successful living, emphasizing insights found in both
conventional and transpersonal psychology and in time-
honored spiritual principles."

Formats:
Books

Topics:
Spirituality

Contact Information:
A Real Human:
Len Finegold
Phone:720-253-5855
Fax: 303-689-9599
E-mail: finegold@connectforjobs.org

The Armarium Press
http://www.thearmariumpress.com
West Hollywood, California, United States

Description:
Publisher of business and educational books and materials, with a current focus on titles that champion the American entrepreneurial spirit.

Formats:
Books

Topics:
Business & Commerce, Careers, Management, Marketing, Small Business

Contact Information:
The Armarium Press
110 Mountain View Drive
New Ipswich, New Hampshire
03071
Telephone (603) 878-3811
Facsimile (603) 878-2227
ArmariumPr@aol.com

Abongold Books Publishing
http://www.abongoldbooks.com
Orangevale, California, United States

Description:
"Publishers of The Crystal Palace, a children's book and Aromatic Blend, a collection of coffee poems"

Formats:
Books

Topics:
Children's Books, Poetry

Contact Information:
Abongold Books Publishing
9444 Erwin Avenue, Suite A
Orangevale, CA 95662

Ad Ventures Publishing
http://www.ad-venturespublishing.com
Blaine, Washington, United States

Description:
A fully searchable yellow pages with the look of a conventional phone book in both print and online. Ad Ventures include web links, video streaming, e-mail links and more

Formats:
Books

Topics:
Business & Commerce, General, Literature, Reference, Travel

Contact Information:
sales@ad-venturespublishing.com
Surrey, British Columbia - Canadian Headquarters
17564 56 A Street Ste 204
Surrey, B.C. V3S 1G3
Phone: (604) 574-2928

Blaine, Washington - Corporate Headquarters
1300 Boblett Street Ste A
PO Box 270
Blaine, Washington 98230
Phone: (360) 332-1939 / 1-877-
561-7772
Fax: (360) 332-6359

Maui, Hawaii - Sales Office
330 Hukilike
Kahului, Hawaii 96732
Phone: (808) 893-2209

Kona, Hawaii - Sales Office
77-6425 Kuakini Hwy Ste D102
Kailua-Kona
808-326-4131
Fax 808-326-4140

Kauai, Hawaii - Sales Office
Lihue, Hawaii
808-245-8839

Honolulu, Hawaii - Sales Office
1132 Bishop Ste 2121
808-551-2284

Advance Books Company

http://www.advancebooks.com
Houston, Texas, United States

Description:
Independent press -- fiction and nonfiction.

Formats:
Books

Topics:
Careers, Cooking, Fiction, Food, Hobbies, How-to,
Humor/Humour, Literature, Multicultural, Mystery,
Nonfiction, Personal Growth, Romance

Contact Information:
staff@advancebooks.com.

AIL NewMedia Publishing

http://www.newmediapublishing.com
Waldwick, New Jersey, United States

Description:
"Publishes books, manuscripts, technical papers, art or literature in print, electronic, audio, video CD-DVD-tape formats."

Formats:
Audio, Booklets, Books, E-Books, E-Books - Adobe Acrobat
PDF, Film/Video, Multimedia CDs, MP3, Music CDs,
Newsletters, PDF, Posters, Software, Technical Papers,
Training Products

Topics:
Biography, General, Information Technology, Self-Help,
Sexuality, Women/Feminism

Contact Information:
AIL NewMedia Publishing
31 Franklin Turnpike
Waldwick, NJ 07463, USA
PH: 201-444-5051

Anhinga Press
http://www.anhinga.org
Tallahassee, Florida, United States

Description:
"Publishes full-length volumes of fine literature, principally poetry."

Formats:
Books

Topics:
Literature, Poetry

Contact Information:
Anhinga Press
P. O. Box 10595
Tallahassee, FL 32302
Phone: (850) 521-9920
Fax: (850) 442-6323
info@anhinga.org

Appletree Press, Inc.
http://www.appletree-press.com
Mankato, Minnesota, United States

Description:
We publish nutrition books & tools that empower people's lives. We have journaling tools, guides and cookbooks that

address diabetes, weight management, heart-health, hypertension and wellness.

Formats:
Booklets, Books

Topics:
Cooking, Food, Medicine, Nutrition, Self-Help

Contact Information:
Appletree Press Inc.
151 Good Counsel Drive Suite 125
Mankato, MN 56001
800.322.5679
507.345.3002 fax
eatwell@hickorytech.net

Ashar Press
http://www.russellsystems.com/ashar/index.htm
San Jose, California, United States
Description:
"Dedicated to Healing Thoughts, Words and Actions."

Formats:
Books

Topics:
Spirituality

Contact Information:
Beverly Breakey Russell, RN,
MFT
PO Box 524,
Galt, CA 95632
1-877-342-7427
Brachabev@aol.com

Asia for Kids
http://www.afk.com/index.tmpl
Location Cincinnati, Ohio, United States

Description:
"Publishes books to CD-ROMs to make the language and culture a living experience for kids of all ages."

Formats:
Books, Multimedia CDs

Topics:
Childcare/Parenting, Language

Contact Information:
info@afk.com

Awe-Struck E-Books
http://www.awe-struck.net
Dubuque, Iowa, United States

Description:
"Dedicated to writing and publishing fine novels, nonfiction, and software at affordable Awe-Struck prices. Our books are available in electronic format, commonly known as electronic books or ebooks."

Formats:
E-Books - Adobe Acrobat PDF, E-Books - Franklin Reader, E-Books - Microsoft Reader, E-Books - Mobipocket Reader, E-Books - Palm, E-Books - Rocket e-book

Contact Information:
tech@awestruckebooks.net

A Gauche Press
http://www.agauchepress.com
San Francisco, California, United States

Description:
Publisher of "Bring the War Home!" a story of a student activist couple testing their relationship and their beliefs as they attempt to organize antiwar Marines in Southern California during the Vietnam War

Formats:
Books, E-Books - Adobe Acrobat e-book

Topics:
Fiction

Contact Information:
2912 Diamond St. #373
San Francisco, CA 94131
Fax: 415.333.6356
bsw@agauchepress.com

Baker Book House
http://www.bakerbooks.com
Grand Rapids, Michigan, United States

Description:
"leading evangelical publisher offering more than 200 releases per year in its five separate divisions"

Formats:
Books

Topics:
Religion/Christian

Basic Educational Materials, Publishers
http://www.bempub.com
Rock Hill, South Carolina, United States

Description:
"Offers quality instructional materials for teachers and special needs professionals in the areas of academic, employment readiness and life skills instruction."

Formats:
Books

Topics:
Childcare/Parenting, Education

Contact Information:
PO Box 36998
Rock Hill, SC 29732-0516
Phone: 803-517-0134
Fax: 803-327-9396
E-mail: bskarlinski@yahoo.com

Beagle Bay Books
http://www.beaglebay.com
Reno, Nevada, United States

Description:
Beagle Bay Books specializes in non-fiction self-help titles for women and women's adventure-romance fiction.

Formats:
Books

Topics:
Fiction, Nonfiction, Personal Growth, Romance, Self-Help, Women/Feminism

Contact Information:
775.827.8654
775.827.8633 fax
info@beaglebay.com

Bison Publishing
http://www.bison.com
Location Carencro, Louisiana, United States

Formats:
Books

Topics:
Business & Commerce

Contact Information:
Ph 952-345-8480
Fax 952-345-8490
inquiries@bison.com

Blue Point Books
http://www.west.net/~bpbooks
Santa Barbara, California, United States

Description:
"Cathy Feldman's series of books about Working Women and find out how to be of comfort with our newest book, One More Star In Heaven Now."

Formats:
Books

Topics:
Women/Feminism

The Book Publishing Company
http://www.bookpubco.com
Summertown, Tennessee, United States

Description:
"Offers books on health and diet, vegetarian cooking, home and garden, and more."

Formats:
Books

Topics:
Children's Books, Cooking, Food, Gardening, Native/ Aboriginal, Sport and Recreation

Contact Information:
Book Publishing Co.
P.O. Box 99
Summertown, TN 38483
888-260-8458
info@bookpubco.com

Cader Publishing Ltd
http://www.cader.com
Sterling Heights, Michigan, United States

Description:
"Sponsor of poetry contests and publisher of anthologies, the web-based International Showcase of Authors, and Verses magazine."

Formats:
Books, Online Information

Topics:
Poetry

Camarillo Publishing Co.
http://www.campubco.com
Anaheim, California, United States

Description:
"Features books on education, direct marketing, credit assistance, and real estate."

Formats:
Books

Topics:
Business & Commerce, Education

Contact Information:
Camarillo Enterprises
P.O. Box 77352
Corona, CA 92877-0111
Voice/Fax: +1.707.221.2001

Carousel Press
http://www.carousel-press.com
Berkeley, California, United States

Description:
"Publishes travel guides, some specifically for families, others; general round-ups on zoos, castle hotels in Europe, and travel in Northern California."

Formats:
Books

Topics:
Families, Travel

Contact Information:
info@carousel-press.com

Cato Institute
http://www.cato.org
Washington, District of Columbia, United States

Description:
"The Cato Institute undertakes an extensive publications program dealing with the complete spectrum of policy issues. Books, monographs, and shorter studies are commissioned to examine the federal budget, Social Security, monetary policy, natural resource policy, military spending, regulation, NATO, international trade, and myriad other issues."

Formats:
Books, Newsletters

Topics:
Business & Commerce

Center For Self Sufficiency
http://www.centerforselfsufficiency.org
Denver, Colorado, United States

Description:
Self-help and how-to site with possibilities for becoming self sufficient.

Formats:
Newsletters, Reports, Training Products

Topics:
Economics, Education, Families, How-to, Self-Help

Contact Information:
Center For Self Sufficiency
P.O. Box 416
Denver, Colorado 80201-0416
303-575-5676
E-mail: info@centerforselfsufficiency.org

Chatoyant
http://www.chatoyant.com
Aptos, California, United States

Description:
Chatoyant publishes short runs of beautifully designed books of poetry.

Formats:
Books

Topics:
Poetry

Devoted To You Books
http://www.devotedtoyoubooks.com/index.php
Wrenshall, Minnesota, United States

Description:
Custom specialty book publisher. Vacation, Kindergarten Graduation, team books, memory albums, Wedding, Baby and collector's editions, childrens 4-colour storybooks. Publish Digital or traditional photos. Earn money while you bless your family with our products.

Formats:
Art Works, Books

Topics:
Careers, Children's Books, Families, Religion/Christian, Self-Publishing

Contact Information:
Phone: 800-704-7250 info@devotedtoyoubooks.com

Eagletree Press
http://www.eagletreepress.com
Eugene, OR, United States

Description:
Midwifery Books including e-books, and other learning resources.

Formats:
Booklets, Books, E-Books, E-Books - Adobe Acrobat e-book, EBooks - Adobe Acrobat PDF, Manuals, PDF, Training Products

Topics:
Education, Families, Medicine, Nursing, Women/Feminism

Contact Information:
Eagletree LLC (DBA Eagletree Press)
P.O. Box 41831
Eugene, OR 97404
E-mail: staff@eagletreepress.com

Emergence Publishing, Inc.
http://www.emergencepub.com
Malverne, New York, United States

Description:
"A book & newsletter publisher dedicated to helping people improve their careers, build a business, manage invest-ments, and develop the skills needed to succeed in this fast changing world."

Formats:
Books

Topics:
Business & Commerce

EquiLibrium Press
http://www.equipress.com
Culver City, California, United States

Description:
"Our vision is to create books that will inspire women to take charge of their physical, spiritual, and emotional well-being."

Formats:
Books

Topics:
Self-Help, Women/Feminism

Contact Information:
10736 Jefferson Blvd. #680
Culver City, California 90230 USA
Ph (310) 204-3290
Fax (310) 204-3550
info@equipress.com

Floating Bridge Press
http://www.scn.org/arts/floatingbridge/main.html
Seattle, Washington, United States

Description:
"A non-profit arts group whose mission is to promote WA State poets by the production of poetry broadsides, chapbooks, and anthologies."

Formats:
Books, Chapbooks

Topics:
Poetry

Contact Information:
floatingbridgepress@yahoo.com

Free Spirit Publishing
http://www.freespirit.com
Minneapolis, Minnesota, United States

Description:
"Award-winning publisher of books and other learning materials for children and teens, parents, educators, counselors, and everyone else who cares about kids."

Formats:
Books

Topics:
Childcare/Parenting, Education

Contact Information:
Free Spirit Publishing
217 Fifth Avenue North, Suite 200
Minneapolis, MN 55401-1299
1-800-735-7323/612-338-2068
612-337-5050 (fax)
help4kids@freespirit.com

Genium Publishing Corporation
http://www.genium.com
Schenectady, New York, United States

Description:
"Publishes information products that are designed to help workers and workplaces function more safely and productively."

Formats:
Books

Topics:
Business & Commerce

Contact Information:
Genium Publishing Corporation
1171 Riverfront Center,
Amsterdam, NY 12010
800-243-6486 518-842-4111
Fax 518-842-1843
e-mail: sales@genium.com

Girl Press
http://girlpress.com/index.htm
Los Angeles, California, United States

Description:
"Dedicated to creating books for girls that will make them strong, self-reliant, and ready for life's adventure. Girl Press backs up this message by donating profits from each book to nonprofit organizations working for girls."

Formats:
Books

Topics:
Children's Books, Women/Feminism

Growing Edge
http://www.growingedge.com
Corvallis, Oregon, United States

Description:
"Publishes a magazine and books about hydroponics, greenhouse culture, aquaponics and other high-tech gardening and agriculture techniques."

Formats:
Books, Magazines

Topics:
Food, Gardening

Contact Information:
The Growing Edge, P.O. Box 1027,
Corvallis, OR USA 97339-1027
USA: (800) 888-6785,
Worldwide: (541) 757-8477,
Fax: (541) 757-0028,

Harbor House Publishers
http://www.harborhouse.com
Boyne City, Michigan, United States
Description:
"Publishes books, visitors guides, annual directories, brochures, newsletters and magazines, including GREAT LAKES/SEAWAY REVIEW, the international transportation magazine of Midcontinent North America."

Formats:
Books, Magazines

Topics:
Travel

Contact Information:
221 Water Street,
Boyne City,
Michigan 49712 USA
(800) 491-1760
(231) 582-2814
fax (231) 582-3392
E-Mail: harbor@harborhouse.com

Harrison House Publishers
http://www.harrisonhouse.com
Tulsa, Oklahoma, United States

Description:
"Publisher of books and gifts for the spirit-filled Christian."

Formats:
Books

Topics:
Religion/Christian

Contact Information:
Physical Address:
2448 E. 81st Street
Suite 4800
Tulsa, OK 74136
Post Office Box:
P. O. Box 35035
Tulsa, OK 74153
Harrison House Main Number:
(800) 888-4126
Harrison House Sales:
(877) 663-1330
Harrison House Sales
(Tulsa,OK)
(918) 523-5700

White Stone Books
(866) 253-8622
Harrison House Sales Fax
(800) 830-5688
Customer Service
(800) 493-2813
customerservice@harrisonhouse.com

Heartsong Books
http://heartsongbooks.com
Blue Hill, Maine, United States

Description:
"Quality books for all ages celebrating the interconnectedness of all life."

Formats:
Books

Topics:
Children's Books, Education, History, Multicultural, Native/Aboriginal, Spirituality, Women/Feminism

Impact Christian Books
http://www.impactchristianbooks.com
Kirkwood, Missouri, United States

Description:
"The major publisher of books on deliverance from demonic spirits, healing and related spiritual self help books. Some of the Best sellers are Pigs in The Parlor, Breaking Unhealthy Soul-Ties, Alive Again!, Ministering to Abortion's Aftermath, Deliverance for Children and Teens, The Acts of Pilate, The Blood Covenant, The Threshold Covenant. All are inspirational and inspiring."

Formats:
Books

Topics:
Religion/Christian

Contact Information:
Impact Christian Books, Inc.
332 Leffingwell Ave., Suite 101,
Kirkwood, MO 63122 USA
Tel. 314-822-3309
Fax 314-822-3325
info@impactchristianbooks.com

Indian Hill Press
http://www.indianhillpress.com
West Tisbury, Massachusetts, United States

Description:
"A small private press dedicated to preserving the art and tradition of fine letterpress printing."

Formats:
Books

Topics:
Poetry

Javan Press
http://www.javanpress.com
Jasper, Georgia, United States

Description:
"Presents self published volumes by Javan. Selected poems available for download."

Formats:
Books, Online Information

Topics:
Poetry

Just Be Publishing, Inc
http://www.justbepublishing.com
Salt Lake City, Utah, United States

Descriptio:
"We publish books designed to fulfill the readers' spiritual search for inner healing and self actualization."

Formats:
Books

Topics:
Spirituality

Contact Information:
bl_ehrler@att.net

King's Harvest
http://www.kingsharvest.com
Seward, Nebraska, United States

Description:
"Christian home schooling materials and curriculum."

Formats:
Books

Topics:
Education, Religion/Christian

Contact Information:
kingsharvest@kingsharvest.com

Kiplinger Books

http://kiplinger.com
Washington, District of Columbia, United States
Description:
"Books and videos on personal finance and business fore-
casting and management from the editors of Kiplinger's
Personal Finance magazine and The Kiplinger Letter."

Formats:
Books

Topics:
Business & Commerce

KISS For Health Publishing

http://www.bookmasters.com/marktplc/00084.htm
Escondido, California, United States

Description:
"Specializes in providing brief, practical and easy-to-use
health and nutrition information."

Formats:
Books

Topics:
Food, Nutrition, Self-Help

Contact Information:
KISS For Health Publishing
P.O. Box 462335-102
Escondido, CA 92046-2335

Krieger Publishing Company
http://www.krieger-publishing.com
Melbourne, Florida, United States

Description:
"A scientific technical book publisher of college and graduate level text and reference books."
Formats:
Books, Multimedia CDs

Topics: Agriculture, Archaeology & Anthropology, Biology, Education, History, Life Sciences, Medicine, Physical Sciences, Physics, Reference, Science, Science Fiction and Fantasy

Contact Information:
Krieger Publishing
P.O. Box 9542
Melbourne, Florida U.S.A.
32902-9542
Phone (321) 724-9542
Fax (321) 951-3671
E-Mail: info@kriegerpublishing.com

LadybugPress
http://www.ladybugbooks.com
San Carlos, California, United States

Description:
At LadybugPress we publish books of interest to women from around the world. We believe that in order for women to become a true force in the world we need, first of all, to talk to each other.

Formats:
Books, Online Information

Topics:
Women/Feminism

London Circle Publishing
http://www.londoncircle.com
Weed, California, United States

Description:
"Publishing electronic books for new, as-yet unpublished authors. There is normally no charge for our publishing service, but authors earn money!"

Formats:
E-Books, E-Books - Adobe Acrobat PDF

Topics:
General

Lone Star Training
http://www.runningarrowfarm.com
Wellington, Texas, United States

Description:
Books on landscape irrigation topics suitable for contractors, homeowners, and others in the Green Industry. Also, selected items on other topics & business videotapes.

Formats:
Booklets, Books, Film/Video, Manuals, Training Products

Topics:
Agriculture, Business & Commerce, How-to, Self-Help, Small Business

Contact Information:
info@runningarrowfarm.com

Lyons Press
http://www.globepequot.com/globepequot
Guilford, Delaware, United States

Description:
"Publisher of fly fishing and hunting books, as well as titles on nature, camping, adventure, general sports, cooking, woodworking, gardening, travel, the sea, history, reference and more."

Formats:
Books

Topics:
Art & Architecture, Cooking, Food, Gardening, History, Maritime, Reference, Sport and Recreation, Travel

Contact Information:
Corporate Headquarters
246 Goose Lane
P.O. Box 480
Guilford, CT 06437
(203)458-4500 Phone
1-888-249-7586 Office
1-800-820-2329 Fax

Main Street Publishing
http://mainstreetpublishing.com
Jackson, Tennessee, United States

Description:
"Promotes writers from West Tennessee. Invites writers to submit their poetry with the possibility of being published."

Formats:
Books

Topics:
Poetry

Contact Information:
editor@mainstreetpublishing.com

Mind Like Water, Inc.
http://www.mindlikewater.com
Overland Park, Kansas, United States

Description:Mind-enhancing e-books, directory and
resources for authors.

Formats:
E-Books - Adobe Acrobat e-book, Multimedia CDs, Online
Information, Newsletters, PDF

Topics:
Business & Commerce, Fiction, Nonfiction, Personal
Finance, Romance

Contact Information:
Mind Like Water, Inc
7419 Metcalf Ave. #321,
Overland Park, KS 66204
913-381-4520
info@mindlikewater.com

NewSage Press, Inc.
http://www.newsagepress.com
Portland, Oregon, United States

Description:
"Publishes non-fiction books that address a myriad of social
concerns, from the animal-human bond to environmental

issues to women's history and more."

Formats:
Books

Topics:
Environment, History, New Age, Pets, Women/Feminism

Contact Information:
NewSage Press, Inc
PO Box 607
Troutdale, OR 97060
Phone 503-695-2211
Toll Free 877-695-2211
Fax 503-695-5406
E mail info@newsagepress.com

Oxford Crest
http://www.oxfordcrest.com
Oxford, Mississippi, United States

Description:
An Oxford, Mississippi-based publisher providing management and marketing guidance to executives, scholars, and
students through informative texts.

Formats:
Books

Topics:
Management, Marketing

Contact Information:
Oxford Crest, Inc
P.O. Box 334
Oxford, MS 38655
800.957.5020 (24-7 pager)
800.957.5025 (fax)

Pinnacle Publishing
http://www.pinpub.com/html/main.isx
Marietta, Georgia, United States

Description:
"A leading provider of newsletters and information products. The two latest additions to the Pinnacle Publishing family of products are Emergency Medicine Practice and IT Recruiter."

Formats:
Magazines, Newsletters

Topics:
Business & Commerce, Medicine

Contact Information:
Pinnacle Publishing
A Division of Lawrence Ragan
Communications, Inc.
316 N. Michigan Avenue, Suite #300
Chicago, IL 60601
Phone: 800-493-4867 x4209
Fax: 312-960-4106
E-mail: pinpub@ragan.com

Pride Publications
http://www.pridepublications.com
Arlington Heights, Illinois, United States

Description:
"We publish case studies on employee empowerment, involvement, leadership, change management and quality. Also, guided driving tours of Colorado, California, New England and other popular destinations."

Formats:
Books

Topics:
Business & Commerce, Travel

Contact Information:
Pride Publications, Inc.
4 N. Wilshire Ln.
Arlington Heights, IL 60004 USA
Fax: 1-847-398-0670
E-mail: ginnodo@pridepublications.com

Rock Dove Publications
http://www.rockdove.com
Silver Lake, Minnesota, United States

Description:
"Christian books and booklets."

Formats:
Booklets, Books

Topics:
Religion/Christian

Comtact Information:
Rock Dove Publications
P.O. Box 203
Silver Lake, MN 55381
Phone: 1(888)HIS-DOVE (orders only)
Phone or Fax: (320)327-2384
orders@rockdove.com
webmaster@rockdove.com

Scepter Publishers Inc
http://www.scepterpublishers.org/product/index.php
Princeton, New Jersey, United States

Description:
"Publishers of Catholic books and bible commentaries."

Formats:
Books

Topics:
Religion/Christian

Contact Information:
Scepter Publishers
P.O. Box 211
New York, NY 10018
Toll Free : 800-322-8773 (US & Canada only)
Tel: 212-354-0670 | Fax: 212-354-0736
e-mail: info@scepterpublishers.org

Silver Lake Publishing
http://www.silverlakepub.com
Los Angeles, California, United States

Description:
"An independent house specializing in personal finance, small business management, risk and insurance, and popular economics. SLP produces books, newsletters, and electronic content for consumers and small businesses."

Formats:
Books, Online Information, Newsletters

Topics:
Business & Commerce, Economics, Law, Personal Finance, Politics

Taking Grades
http://www.takinggrades.com
Conover, North Carolina, United States

Formats:
Books

Topics:
Education, Childrens

Contact Information:
takinggrades@charter.net

UglyTown Productions
http://www.uglytown.com/console.html
Los Angeles, California, United States

Description:
Independent publishing house offering neo-pulp mysteries and original fiction.

Formats:
Books

Topics:
Fiction, Mystery

Contact Information:
UglyTown
2148 1/2 Sunset Blvd Ste 204
Los Angeles CA 90026
voice: 213 484 8334
fax: 213 484 8333
uglytom@UglyTown.com

Valentine Publishing Group
http://www.vpg.net
Palmdale, California, United States

Formats:
Books

Topics:
General

Contact Information:
Valentine Publishing Group
18543 Devonshire St. #458
Northridge, CA 91324
(818) 366-8698 ph
(818) 831-6659 fx
pubservices@vpg.net

Warner Books
http://www.twbookmark.com
New York, New York, United States

Formats:
Books

Topics:
General

Contact Information:
10 Cadillac Drive, Suite 220,
Brentwood, TN 37027
Phone: 615-221-0996 ext.221.
Fax: 615-221-0962.

Yardbird Books
http://www.yardbird.com
Airville, Pennsylvania, United States

Description:
"Features challenging, well-made books of fiction, non-fiction, and poetry".

Formats:
Books

Topics:
Fiction, Poetry

Contact Information:
Yardbird Books P.O. Box 5333
Harrisburg, PA 17110
1-800-622-6044 or 717-927-6377
info@yardbird.com

YogaVidya.com
http://www.yogavidya.com
Woodstock, New York, United States

Description:
YogaVidya.com is dedicated to publishing excellent and affordable books about Yoga. It is independent of all other commercial, governmental, educational, and religious institutions.

Formats:
Books, PDF

Topics:
New Age, Personal Growth, Philosophy, Religion/Hinduism, Spirituality

Contact Information:
YogaVidya.com
PO Box 569
Woodstock, NY 12498-0569 USA
fax 586-283-4680
info@yogavidya.com

York Press
http://www.yorkpress.com
Timonium, Maryland, United States

Description:
"Publisher of books about language development and disabilities, especially dyslexia, and about hearing impairment."

Formats:
Books

Topics:
Language, Medicine

Contact Information:
York Press, Inc.
PO Box 504
Timonium, MD 21094
Toll-free: 1-800-962-2763
Fax: 410 560-6758
E-mail: info@yorkpress.com

Zipper Press, Inc
http://www.zipperpress.com
Dayton, Ohio, United States

Description:
"Creating quality books to meet the high standards set for children by parents, grandparents, teachers, librarians, family, and friends."

Formats:
Books

Topics:
Children's Books

Contact Information:
Zipper Press
P. O. Box 90125
Dayton, OH 45490-0125

Chapter Thirty-Nine
Magazines
to Sell Your Work

Directory of magazines in a variety of different topic areas should you wish to sell your work in this way.

Magazine Name
Address
Phone, Fax
E-mail, Web site
Contact

Writer Field: Animals

Animal Watch
315 E 62nd St New York, NY 10021
212-876-7700 212-410-0087
editor@aspca.org www.aspca.org
Marion Lance

Cat Fancy, Cat Care for Responsible Owner
Box 6050, Mission Viejo, CA 92690
949-855-8822 n/a
n/a www.catfancy.com
Keith Bush

Dog Fancy
Box 6050, Mission Viejo, CA 92690-6050
949-855-3045 n/a
sbiller@fancypubs.com www.dogfancy.com
Steven Biller

Pet Life - Your Companion Animal Magazine
3451 Boston Ave, Forth Worth, TX 76116
817-560-6100, 817-560-6196
awilson@mmqweb.com www.petlifeweb.com
Alexis Wilson

Writer Field: Business & Finance

Entrepreneur Magazine, page 400-419
2445 McCabe Way, Irvine, CA 92614
949-261-2325, 949-261-0234
entmag@entrepreneur.com www.entrepreneur.com
Peggy Reeves

Bennett Profit, The Magazine for Canadian Entrepreneurs
777 Bay St, 5th Floor, Toronto, ON M5W 1A7
416-596-5016, 416-596-5111
profit@profitmag.ca www.profitguide.com
Ian Portsmouth

Report On Business Magazine
444 Front St W, Toronto, ON M5V 2S9
416-585-5499, n/a
robmag@globeandmail.ca www.robmagnet.com
Susan Macphail

Business London
1174 Gainsburough Rd, London, ON N5Y 4X3
519-472-7601, 519-473-7859
n/a, n/a
Gord Delamont

In Business Windsor
1614 Lesperance Rd, Tecumseh, ON N8N 1Y3
519-735-2080, 519-735-2082
inbiz2@mnsi.net www.inbizwin.com
Gordon Hillman

Utah Business The Magazine for Decision Makers
85 E Fort Union Blvd, Midvale UT 84047-153
801-568-0114, n/a
editor@utahbusiness.com www.utahbusiness.com
Gail Newbold

Writer Field: Child Care and Parenting

All About Kids Magazine
417-428 101-1077 Celestial St, Cincinnati, OH 45202
513-684-050, 513-684-0507
editor@aak.com www.aak.com
Tom Wynne

At–Home Mother
406 E Buchanan Ave, Fairfield, IA 52556-3810
n/a, n/a
editor@athomemothers.com www.athomemothers.com
Jeanette Lisefski

Baby Talk
429-430 530 Fifth Ave, 4th Floor, New York, NY 10036
212-522-8989, 212-522-8750
n/a, www.babytalk.com
Brittni Boyd

Child
375 Lexington Ave, New York, NY 10017-5514
212-499-2000, 212-499-2038
childmag@aol.com www.child.com
Submissions

Christian Parenting Today
465 Gundersen Dr, Carol Stream, IL 60188-2489
630-260-6200, 630-260-0114
cpt@christianparenting.net   n/a
Lori Fedele

Expecting
37 Hanna Ave, Suite 1, Toronto, ON M6K 1W9
416-537-2604, 416-538-1794
n/a, n/a
Tracy Hitchcock

Family Life
530 Fifth Ave, New York, NY 10036
212-522-6240, 212-467-1248
family_life@timeinc.com www.familylifemag.com
Jacqueline Leigh Ross

Today's Parent Pregnancy & Birth
269 Richmond St. W, Toronto, ON M5V 1X1
416-596-8680, 416-596-1991
n/a, www.todaysparent.com
Editor

Working Mother Magazine
135 W 50th St, 16th Floor, New York, NY 10020-1201
212-445-6100, 212-445-6174
editors@workingmother.com www.workingmother.com
Articles Department

Writer Field: Consumer Service & Business Opportunity

Home Business Magazine
9582 Hamilton Ave, PMB 368 Huntington Beach, CA 92646
n/a, 714-962-7722
henderso@ix.netcom.com www.homebusinessmag.com
Stacy Henderson

Money Saving Ideas
320 Valley St, Burlington, IA 52601
319-752-5415, 319-752-3421
n/a, n/a
Nancy Heinzel

Spare Time Magazine
2400 S Commerce Dr, New Berlin, WI 53151
262-780-1070, 262-780-1071
editor@sparetime.com   www.sparetimemagazine.com
n/a

Writer Field: Contemporary Culture

Book Club Today
Box 210165, Cleveland, OH 44121-7165
n/a, 216-382-0644
bookclubtoday@aol.com   www.bookclubtoday.com
BonnieEaver

Bookpage
2143 Belcourt Ave, Nashville, TN 37212
615-292-8926, 615-292-8249
lynn@bookpage.com   www.bookpage.com
Ms. Lynn L. Green

Boston Review
E53-407 MIT, Cambridge, MA 02139
617-253-3642, n/a
bostonreview@mit.edu   www.bostonreview.mit.edu
Jefferson Decker

Common Ground
201-3091 W Broadway, Vancouver, BC V6K 2G9
604-733-2215, 604-733-4415
editor@commongroundmagazine.com, n/a
RobertScheer

FW Magazine
302-296 Richmond St West, Toronto, ON M5V 1X2
416-591-6537, 416-591-2390
angela@myfw.com   www.myfw.com
P.J. Tarasuk

The Women's Review of Books
106 Central St, Wellesley, MA 02481
n/a, n/a
n/a, www.wellesley.edu/womensreview
LindaGardiner

Yes!, A Journal of Positive Futures
Box 10818, Bainbridge Island, WA 98110
206-842-0216, 206-842-5208
editors@futurenet.org   www.futurenet.org
Carol Estes

Writer Field: Disabilities

Abilities
501-489 College St, Toronto, ON M6G 1A5
416-923-1885, 416-923-9829
able@abilities.ca www.abilities.ca
Lisa Bendall

Accent On Living
Box 700, Bloomington, IL 61702-0700
309-378-2961, 309-378-4420
acntlvng@aol.com www.accentonliving.com
Betty Garee

Arthritis Today
1330 W Peachtree St, Atlanta, GA 30309
404-872-7100, 404-872-9559
atmail@arthritis.org www.arthritis.org
Michele Taylor

Writer Field: General Interest

Reader's Digest (Canada)
476-86 1100 Rene-Levesque Blvd W, Montreal, QC H3B 5H5
514-940-0751, n/a
n/a, www.readersdigest.ca
Ron Starr

Readers Review
320 Valley St, Burlington, IA 52601
319-752-5415, 319-752-3421
n/a, n/a
Nancy Heinzel

The Saturday Evening Post
1100 Waterway Blvd, Indianapolis, IN 46202
317-636-8881, 317-637-0126
satevepst@aol.com www.satvevpst.org
Patrick Perry

The Sun, A Magazine of Ideas
107 N Roberson St, Chapel Hill, NC 27516
919-942-5282 n/a
n/a, www.thesunmagazine.org
Sy Safransky

Troika, Wit, Wisdom & Wherewithal
Box 1006, Weston, CT 06883
203-319-0873, 203-319-0755
submit@troikamagazine.com www.troikamagazine.com
Celia Meadow

The World & I
3600 New York Ave NE, Washington, DC 20002
202-635-4000, 202-269-9353
editor@worldandimag.com www.worldandi.com
Gary Rowe

Writer Field: Health & Fitness

Better Heath
1450 Chapel St, New Haven, CT 06511-4440
203-789-3972, 203-789-4053
n/a, n/a
Cynthia Wolfe Boynton

Delicious Living
1401 Pearl St, Suite 200, Boulder, CO 80302
n/a, n/a
delicious@newhope.com www.healthwell.com
Lara Evans

Fit
1700 Broadway, 34th Floor, New York, NY 10019
212-541-7100, 212-245-1241
n/a, n/a
Rita Trieger

Fitness Magazine
375 Lexington Ave, New York, NY 10017-5514
212-499-2000, 212-499-1568
n/a, n/a
Liz Vaccariello

Men's Health
33 E Minor St, Emmaus, PA 18098
610-967-5171, 610-967-7725
tedspiker@rodale.com www.menshealth.com
Ted Spiker

Muscle & Fitness
21100 Erwin St, Woodland Hills, CA 91367
818-884-6800, 818-595-0463
n/a, www.muscle-fitness.com
Vincent Scalisi

Natural Health
70 Lincoln St, 5th Floor, Boston, MA 02111
617-753-8900, 617-457-0966
naturalhealth@weiderpub.com
www.naturalhealthmag.com
Maria Mandile

New Living
1212 Rt. 25A Suite 1B, Stony Brook, NY 11790
631-751-8819, 631-751-8910
newliving@aol.com www.newliving.com
Christine Lynn Harvey

Shape Magazine
21100 Erwin St, Woodland Hills, CA 91367
818-595-0593, 818-704-7620
n/a, www.shapemag.com
Anne Russell

The Walking Magazine
45 Bromfield St, Boston, MA 02108
617-574-0076, 617-338-7433
letters@walkingmag.com www.walkingmag.com
Catherine Croteau

Your Health & Fitness
900 Skokie Blvd, Northbrook, IL 60062-1574
847-205-3000, 847-564-8197
n/a, n/a
Debb Bastian

Writer Field: Home & Garden

Better Homes & Gardens
1716 Locust St, Des Moines, IA 50309-3023
515-284-3044, 515-284-3763
n/a, www.bhg.com
Laura O'Neill

Birds & Blooms
5925 Country Lane, Greendale, WI 53129
n/a, n/a
editors@birdsandblooms.com www.birdsandblooms.com
Jeff Nowak

Canadian Home Workshop
340 Ferrier St, Suite 210, Markham, ON L3R 2Z5
905-475-8440, 905-475-9246
letters@canadianhomeworkshop.com
Douglas Thomson

Country Home
1716 Locust St, Des Moines, IA 50309-3023
515-284-2015, 515-284-2552
countryh@mdp.com   www.countryhomemagazine.com
Melissa Manning

Country Living
224 W 57th St, New York, NY 10019
212-649-3509, n/a
n/a, n/a
Marjorie Gage

Decorating Ideas
1633 Broadway, New York, NY 10019
212-767-6000, 212-767-5612
n/a, n/a
Amanda Rock

Flower and Garden Magazine
51 Kings Highway W, Haddonfield, NJ 08033-2114
856-354-5034, 856-354-5147
kcpublishing@earthlink.net
www.flowerandgardenmag.com
Senior Editor

Home Digest
268 Lakeshore Rd E, Unit 604, Oakville, ON L6J 7S4
905-844-3361, 905-849-4618
homedigest@canada.com   www.home-digest.com
William Roebuck

Writer Field: Young Girls & Boys

Discoveries
6401 The Paseo, Kansas City, MO 64131
816-333-7000 ext 2728, 816-333-4439
n/a, n/a
Katherine Hendrixson

Girl's Life
4517 Harford Rd, Baltimore, MD 21214
410-254-0991 n/a
n/a, www.girlslife.com
Kelly A. White

Highlights For Children
803 Church St, Honesdale, PA 18431-1824
570-253-1080, n/a
n/a, n/a
Beth Troop

Hopscotch
Box 164, Bluffton, OH 45817-0164
419-358-4610 n/a
n/a, www.hopscotchmagazine.com
Virginia Edwards

Humpty Dumpty's Magazine
Box 567, Indianapolis, IN 46206-0567
317-636-8881 n/a
n/a, n/a
Nancy S. Axelrad

Jack And Jill
Box 567, Indianapolis, IN 46206-0567
317-636-8881, 317-684-8094
n/a, n/a
Daniel Lee

Ladybug
Box 300, Peru, IL 61354-0300
815-224-6656, n/a
n/a, n/a
Paula Morrow

Owl Magazine
179 John St, Suite 500, Toronto, ON M5T 3G5
416-340-2700, 416-340-9769
owl@owl.on.ca www.owlkids.com
Mary Beth Leatherdale

Turtle Magazine For Preschool Kids
Box 567, Indianapolis, IN 46206-0567
317-636-8881, 317-684-8094
n/a, www.turtlemag.com
Ms. Terry Harshman

Writer Field: Poetry and Writers' Short Stories

ARC, Canada's National Poetry Magazine
549-559---568 Box 7368, Ottawa, ON K1L 8E4
n/a, n/a
n/a, n/a
John Barton or Rita Donovan

B & A New Fiction
Box 702, Station P, Toronto, ON M5S 2Y4
416-822-8708, n/a
bloodaphorisms@hotmail.com, n/a
Sam Hiyate

Bellingham Review
Mail Stop 9053, Western Washington University
Bellingham, WA 98225
360-650-4863, n/a
bhreview@cc.wwu.edu www.wwu.edu/~bhreview editor

Chicken Soup For The Soul
Box 30880, Santa Barbara, CA 93130
805-682-6311, 805-563-2945
nautio@chickensoup.com www.chickensoup.com
Nancy Mitchell-Autio

The Connecticut Poetry Review
Box 818, Stonington, CT 06378
n/a, n/a
n/a, n/a
J. Claire White

Creative Nonfiction
5501 Walnut St, Suite 202, Pittsburgh, PA 15232
412-688-0304, 412-683-9173
info@creativenonfiction.org   www.creativenonfiction.org
Lee Gutkind

Dreams & Visions New Frontiers in Christian Fiction
35 Peter St S, Orillia, ON L3V 5A8
705-329-1770, 705-329-1770
skysong@bconnex.net www.bconnex.net/~skysong
Steve Stanton

Field, Contemporary Poetry & Poetics
10 N Professor St, Oberlin, OH 44074-1095
440-775-8408, 440-775-8124
oc.press@oberlin.edu www.oberlin.edu/~ocpress
Linda Slocum

Futures Magazine
3039-38th Ave, Minneapolis, MN 55406-2140
612-724-4023, n/a
babs@suspenseunlimited.net   www.futuresforstorylovers.com
Babs Lakey

Grain Literary Magazine
Box 1154, Regina, SK S4P 3B4
306-244-2828, 306-244-0255
grain.mag@sk.sympatico.ca   www.skwriter.com
Elizabeth Philips

The Journal
421 Denney Hall, 164 W 17th Ave, Columbus, OH 43210
614-292-4076, 614-292-7816
thejournal105@postbox.acs.ohio-state.edu
www.cohums.ohiostate.edu/english/journals/the_journal/
Homepage.htm
Ellen Levy

The Prairie Journal of Canadian Literature
Box 61203, Brentwood Postal Services, 217K-3630
Brentwood Rd, Calgary, AB T2L 2K6
n/a, n/a
prairiejournal@iname.com   www.geocities.com/prairiejournal
A. Burke

Writer Field: Men's

Esquire
578-580 250 W 55th St, New York, NY 10019
212-649-4020, n/a
n/a, n/a
A. J. Jacobs

GC Magazine
Box 331775, Fort Worth, TX 76136
817-654-2334, 817-457-5298
bellbrook@flash.net www.gc-magazine.com
Jon Keeyes

Men's Journal
1290 Avenue of the Americas, New York, NY 10104-0298
212-484-1616, 212-767-8213
n/a, www.mensjournal.com
Taylor A. Plimpton

UMM Urban Male Magazine
6 Antares Dr, Phase 1, Unit 7, Nepean, ON K2E 8A9
613-723-6216, n/a
editor@umm.ca www.umm.ca David Sachs

Writer Field: Self Improvement

Personal Journaling Magazine
605-606 1507 Dana Ave, Cincinnati, OH 45207
n/a, 513-531-2902
journaling@fwpubs.com   www.journalingmagazine.com
Editor

Psychology Today
49 E 21st St, 11th Floor, New York, NY 10010
212-260-7210, 212-260-7445
psychtoday@aol.com www.psychologytoday.com
CarinGorrell

Writer Field: Travel

Sunset Magazine
608-620 80 Willow Rd, Menlo Park, CA 94025-3691
650-321-3600, 650-327-7537
travelquery@sunset.com www.sunsetmagazine.com
Peter Fish

Village Profile
33 N Geneva, Elgin, IL 60120
800-600-0134 ext 221, n/a
vp_editorial@ameritech.net   www.villageprofile.com
David Gall

Yankee
Box 520, Dublin, NH 03444-0520
603-563-8111, 603-563-8252
queries@yankeepub.com www.newengland.com
Ms Sam Darley
Alaska, Exploring Life on the Last Frontier
619 E Ship Creek Ave, Suite 329, Anchorage, AK 99501
907-272-6070, 907-258-5360
n/a, www.alaskamagazine.com
Donna Rae Thompson

Arizona Foothills Magazine
8132 N 87th Place, Scottsdale, AZ 85258
480-460-5203, 480-443-1517
reneedee@azfoothillsmag.com   www.azfoothillsmagazine.com
Shannon Bartlett

Carefree Enterprise Magazine
Box 1145, Carefree, AZ 85377
n/a, n/a
staff@carefreeenterprise.com
www.carefreeenterprise.com Susan Smyth

Los Angeles Times Magazine
202 W First St, Los Angeles, CA 90012
213-237-7811, 213-237-7386
n/a, n/a
Alice Short

Palm Springs Life
303 N Indian Canyon, Palm Springs, CA 92262
760-325-2333, 760-325-7008
n/a, n/a
Sarah Hagerty

Aspen Magazine
720 E Durant Ave, Suite E-8, Aspen, CO 81612
970-920-4040, 970-920-4044
edit@aspenmagazine.com www.aspenmagazine.com
Jamie Miller

Connecticut Magazine
35 Nutmeg Dr, Trumbull, CT 06611
203-380-6600, 203-380-6610
n/a, www.connecticutmag.com
Dale Salm

The Washington Post
1150-15th St NW, Washington, DC 20071
202-334-7750, 202-334-1069
n/a, n/a
K.C. Summers

Florida Living Magazine
102 Drennen Rd, Suite C-5, Orlando, FL 32806
407-816-9596, 407-816-9373
editor@flaliving.com www.floridamagazine.com
KristenCifers

Writer Field: Religious

Bible Advocate
660-668 Box 33677, Denver, CO 80233
303-452-7973, n/a
bibleadvocate@cog7.org/ba/ www.cog7.org/ba
Sherri Langton

Catholic Digest
2115 Summit Ave, St Paul, MN 55105-1081
651-962-6739, 651-962-6758
cdigest@stthomas.edu www.catholicdigest.org
Articles Editor

The Christian Century
104 S Michigan Ave, Suite 700, Chicago, IL 60605-1150
312-263-7510, 312-263-7540
n/a, www.christiancentury.org
David Heim

Christian Courier
4-261 Martindale Rd, St. Catharines, ON L2W 1A1
905-682-8311, 905-682-8313
cceditor@aol.com, n/a
Harry Der Nederlanden

Christian Home & School
3350 E Paris Ave SE, Grand Rapids, MI 49512
616-957-1070 ext 239, 616-957-5022
rogers@csionline.org www.csionline.org/chs
Roger Schmurr

Christian Reader
465 Gundersen Dr, Carol Stream, IL 60188
630-260-6200, 630-260-0114
creditor@christianreader.net www.christianreader.net
Cynthia Thomas

Christian Social Action
100 Maryland Ave NE, Washington, DC 20002
202-488-5631, 202-488-1617
ealsgaard@umc-gbcs.org, n/a
Erik Alsgaard

Christianity Today
465 Gundersen Dr, Carol Stream, IL 60188-2498
630-260-6200, 630-260-8428
cteditor@christianitytoday.com www.christianitytoday.com
Mark Galli

Decision
1300 Harmon Place, Minneapolis, MN 55403-1988
612-338-0500, 612-335-1299
submissions@bgea.org www.decisionmag.org
Bob Paulson

Discipleship Journal
Box 35004, Colorado Springs, CO 80935-0004
719-531-3514, 719-598-7128
sue.kline@navpress.com   www.discipleshipjournal.com
Sue Kline

The Door
Box 1444, Waco, TX 76703-1444
214-827-2625, 254-752-4915
rfd3@flash.net   www.thedoormagazine.com
Robert Darden

Evangel
Box 535002, Indianapolis, IN 46253-5002
317-244-3660, n/a
n/a, n/a
Julie Innes

The Evangelical Baptist
18 Louvigny, Lorraine, QC J6Z 1T7
450-621-3248, 450-621-0253
eb@fellowship.ca www.fellowship.ca
Ginette Cotnoir

Evangelizing Today's Child
Box 348, Warrenton, MO 63383-0348
636-456-4321, 636-456-4321
etceditor@cefinc.org   www.cefinc.org/etcmag
Elsie Lippy

Expression
Box 44148, Pittsburgh, PA 15205-0348
412-920-5547, 412-920-5549
editor@expressionnews.org   www.expressionnews.org
CathyHickling

Faith Today
Box 3745, Markham, ON L3R 0Y4
905-479-5885, 905-479-4742
ft@efc-canada.com www.efc-canada.com
Bill Fledderus

Forward In Christ
2929 N Mayfair Rd, Milwaukee, WI 53222-4398
414-256-3888, 414-256-3899
fic@sab.wels.net www.wels.net
Gary P. Baumler

Light and Life Magazine
Box 535002, Indianapolis, IN 46253-5002
317-244-3660, 317-248-9055
llmauthors@fmcna.org, n/a
Doug Newton

The Living Church
816 E Juneau Ave, Box 514036, Milwaukee, WI 53203
414-276-5420, 414-276-7483
tlc@livingchurch.org, n/a
David Kalvelage

The Lookout
8121 Hamilton Ave, Cincinnati, OH 45231-9981
513-931-4050, 513-931-0950
lookout@standardpub.com www.standardpub.com
Shawn McMullen

The Lutheran
8765 W Higgins Rd, Chicago, IL 60631-4183
773-380-2540, 773-380-2751
lutheran@elca.org www.thelutheran.org
David L. Miller

The Lutheran Digest
Box 4250, Hopkins, MN 55343
952-933-2820, 952-933-5708
tldi@lutherandigest.com www.lutherandigest.com
David L.Tank

Message Magazine
55 West Oak Ridge Dr, Hagerstown, MD 21740
301-393-4099, 301-393-4103
message@rhpa.org   www.messagemagazine.org
Pat Sparks Harris

Our Family
Box 249, Battleford, SK S0M 0E0
306-937-7771, 306-937-7644
n/a, www.ourfamilymagazine.com
Marie-Louise Ternier-Gommers

The Pentecostal Messenger
Box 850, Joplin, MO 64802-0850
417-624-7050, 417-624-7102
johnm@pcg.org   www.pcg.org
John Mallinak

Presbyterians Today
100 Witherspoon St, Louisville, KY 40202-1396
502-569-5637, 502-569-8632
today@pcusa.org www.pcusa.org/today
Eva Stimson

Preserving Christian Homes
8855 Dunn Rd, Hazelwood, MO 63042
314-837-7304, 314-837-4503
youth@upci.org   www.upci.org/youth
Todd Gaddy

Prism Magazine
10 E Lancaster Ave, Wynnewood, PA 19096
610-645-9391, 610-649-8090
kristyn@esa-online.org www.esa-online.org
Kristyn Komarnicki

Purpose
616 Walnut Ave, Scottdale, PA 15683-1999
724-887-8500, 724-887-3111
horsch@mph.org www.mph.org
James E. Horsch

Signs Of The Times
Box 5353, Nampa, ID 83653-5353
208-465-2579, 208-465-2531
mmoore@pacificpress.com n/a
Marvin Moore

Together
Box 656 Route 2, Grottoes, VA 24441
n/a, n/a
tgether@aol.comn n/a
Melodie M. Davis

The United Church Observer
478 Huron St, Toronto, ON M5R 2R3
416-960-8500, 416-960-8477
general@ucobserver.org www.ucobserver.org
Muriel Duncan

The Upper Room
Box 340004, Nashville, TN 37203-0004
615-340-7252, 615-340-7267
theupperroommagazine@upperroom.org www.upperroom.org
Marilyn Beaty

Whispers From Heaven
7373 N Cicero, Lincolnwood, IL 60712
n/a, 847-329-5387
n/a, n/a
Acquisitions Editor

Woman's Touch
1445 Boonville Ave, Springfield, MO 65802-1894
417-862-2781, 417-862-0503
womanstouch@ag.org www.ag.org/womanstouch
Darla Knoth

World Christian
Box 1357, Oak Park, IL 60304
708-524-5070, 708-524-5174
winpress7@aol.com, n/a
Phillip Huber

World Pulse
Box 794, Wheaton, IL 60189
630-752-7158, 630-752-7155
pulsenews@aol.com   www.wheaton.edu/bgc/emis
Editor

Writer Field: Retirement
Alive
Box 46464, Cincinnati, OH 45246-0464
513-825-3681, n/a
n/a, n/a
A. June Lang

Modern Maturity
601 E St NW, Washington, DC 20049
202-434-6880, n/a
n/a, www.aarp.org
Hugh Delehanty

Plus
3565 S Higuera St, San Luis Obispo, CA 93401
805-544-8711, 805-544-4450
plusmag@fix.net, n/a
George Brand

Writer Field: Teen and Young Adults

Campus Life
758-764 465 Gundersen Dr, Carol Stream, IL 60188
630-260-6200, 630-260-0114
clmag@campuslife.com www.campuslife.net
Amber Penney

Guideposts For Teens
Box 638, Chesterton, IN 46304
219-929-4429, 219-926-3839
gp4t@guideposts.org www.gp4teens.com
Betsy Kohn

Insight
55 W Oak Ridge Dr, Hagerstown, MD 21740
n/a, n/a
insight@rhpa.org   www.insightmagazine.org
Lori Peckham

Listen Magazine
55 W Oak Ridge Dr, Hagerstown, MD 21740
301-393-4019, 301-393-4055
listen@healthconnection.org, n/a
Anita Jacobs

Live
1445 N Boonville Ave, Springfield, MO 65802-1894
417-862-2781, 417-862-6059
rl-live@gph.org www.radiantlife.org
Paul W. Smith

MH-18 Fitness,Sports, Girls, Gear, Life
400 S 10th St, Emmaus, PA 18049
n/a, 610-967-7725
n/a, www.mh-18.com
Jenny Everett

Seventeen
850 Third Ave, New York, NY 10022
212-407-9700, 212-407-9899
n/a, www.seventeen.com
Tamara Glenny

Today's Christian Teen
Box 100, Morgantown, PA 19543
610-913-0796, 610-913-0797
tcpubs@mkpt.com, n/a
Elaine Williams

What Magazine
108-93 Lombard Ave, Winnipeg, MB R3B 3B1
204-985-8160, 204-957-5638
l.malkin@m2ci.mb.ca, n/a
Leslie Malkin

Writer Field: Women's

Complete Woman
783-789 875 N Michigan Ave, Suite 3434,
Chicago, IL 60611-1901
312-266-8680, n/a
n/a, n/a
Lora Wintz

Cosmopolitan
224 W 57th St, New York, NY 10019
212-649-2000, n/a
n/a, n/a
Michele Promaulayko

Country Woman
5400 South 60th St, Greendale, WI 53129
414-423-0100, n/a
n/a, n/a
Kathleen Anderson

Family Circle Magazine
375 Lexington Ave, New York, NY 10017-5514
212-499-2000, 212-499-1987
nclark@familycircle.com   www.familycircle.com
Nancy Clark

Modern Bride
249 W 17th St, New York, NY 10011
212-462-3472, 212-367-8342
n/a, www.modernbride.com
Christina Cush

More Magazine
125 Park Ave, New York, NY 10017
212-455-1433, n/a
n/a, www.lhj.com/more
Stephanie Woodard

Moxie Magazine
1230 Glen Ave,Berkeley, CA 94708
510-540-5510, n/a
emily@moxiemag.com www.moxiemag.com
Emily Hancock

Ms Magazine
20 Exchange Place, 22nd Floor, New York, NY 10005
212-509-2092, 212-509-2407
info@msmagazine.com www.msmagazine.com
Manuscripts Editor

Redbook Magazine
224 W 57th St, New York, NY 10019
n/a, n/a
n/a, n/a
Editor

Today's Christian Woman
465 Gundersen Dr, Carol Stream, IL 60188-2498
630-260-6200, 630-260-0114
tcwedit@christianitytoday.com
www.todayschristianwoman.net
Ginger Kolbaba

Woman's Day
1633 Broadway, 42nd Floor, New York, NY 10019
212-767-6000, 212-767-5610
n/a, www.womansday.com
Jane Chesnutt

Women In Business
9100 Ward Pkwy, Box 8728, Kansas City, MO 64114-0728
816-361-6621, 816-361-4991
abwa@abwaq.org www.abwa.org
Rachel Warbington

Check Out

Our New

Bookstore

www.yourchoicebooks.info

Section Eight:

32 Tips, Tricks and Techniques for Authors

Chapter Forty

1. Business Book Reviewer: a great testimonial and reviews for business books at
    American Institute of Small Business
    925 545 7001
    www.aisb.biz

Get a great review from them!!

2. Best time to approach book clubs is in the manuscript phase. Although once you have a small print run many will accept this too. They like new books.

3. Another way of making money writing is being a writer for "fan clubs". Somebody has to do it, why not you?

4. Have you ever heard of bed books? Check it out at
    http://bedbooks.net/index.html

5. Writer's competitions and grants:
    www.writersdigest.com

6. Vanity press means they say they are a publisher but make you pay.

7. Traditional publishers take no money from you. They may not give you a royalty up front; they may ask you to wait until the books sell.

8. Put an order form in the back of your book to sell your other books.

9. Think about getting into a catalogue... Joint Venture with them to sell books. Ask yourself what your subject is. Are there companies that cater to your target market? Here's a secret... the answer is YES! www.shop.com or www.catalogsite.com, for a list of catalogues and to search by topic.

10. Do up postcards with your website and put them up on cork boards, leave on networking tables, etc. Word of mouth sells.

11. What about museums? Does your book fall into the following categories? Tourism, antiques, animals, sports, plants, crafts, art history, nature...

12. You might want to touch base with BookWire to announce your book tour. This website lets everyone know where you will be: www.bookwire.com

13. Have something "visual" when you are doing your book signing. For myself I do a free keynote: "Self Publishing Made Easy"... I have a manuscript in paper form printed from the computer. I have a proof and cover. I have the final copy of the book. This shows the three stages of printing. What do you have that can be visual?

14. We use Blitzprint for small print runs. Check out their website at: http://www.blitzprint.com - tell them Kathleen Mailer sent you!

15. For large print runs, check out
    http://www.houghtonboston.com

16. Define your book in 25 words or less to help you sell it and help the media sell it when they have a short blast of time. Mine? "It's a treasure trove encompassing all aspects of writing, self publishing and marketing for authors so that they can explode their income and create a global buzz!"

17. Write your own book review so that it's easier for smaller media venues to use.

18. Hold a draw at your book signing to gather names to keep your readers posted. Send them an "e-card" or postcard thanking them.
    See e-cards at www.bluemountain.com

19. 19. I often get questions about "Who owns copyright?" or "How much of someone else's can I use?" Go to http://www.copyright.gov for U.S. or http://cipo.gc.ca for Canadian copyright for more information.

20. Make sure your title gives a benefit to your reader. Pain or Gain are good examples. Solve a problem.

21. Go to the world's biggest bookstore, www.amazon.com, to find out if your title has already been selected by another author.

22. Think about writing your book in another language and sending it to another country.

23. Don't use the direct mail approach if your book is less than $30. Add several books together to make a larger priced item.

24. Decide to help a charity and joint venture with them. 10% of your sales can go to charity... I did this with the Literacy Foundation. It was fun and profitable.

25. SPAN-USA- Small Publishing Association of North America. Maybe you might want to join? http://www.spannet.org

26. IPAC-CANADA- another great venue. Independent Publishers Asociation of Canada at http://www.ipac-publishers.com

27. Hold a contest! Gather names for your database and get in the media!

28. Make sure you have your contact information on EVERY page you send out.

29. Authors hang out with other authors. Know a bunch? Write your own catalogue and share customers.

30. To sell your book, make an offer they can't refuse. Give them bonus material like eBooks, or special reports that cost you nothing to manufacture but add at least 10 times the amount of value to your book.

31. What about a book singing in a local grocery store or at WalMart? Ask Ask Ask.

32. Just because a store doesn't sell books now doesn't mean you shouldn't approach them. Example: jewelery store? You have a bridal book about planning your wedding? AHA... that is what I'm talkin' about!

Contact Information:

Kathleen D. Mailer
#44 Bernard Way NW,
Calgary, Alberta T3K 2E9
403-230-5946 ext 3
mastersmentor@shaw.ca

www.howtowriteandpublish.com
www.kathleenmailer.com
www.yourchoicebooks.info